I0421000

Editor-in-Chief and Founder:
   Lyndon H. LaRouche, Jr.
Editorial Board: *Lyndon H. LaRouche, Jr. , Helga Zepp-LaRouche, Paul Gallagher, Tony Papert, Gerald Rose, Dennis Small, Jeffrey Steinberg, William Wertz*
Co-Editors: *Paul Gallagher, Tony Papert*
Managing Editor: *Nancy Spannaus*
Technology: *Marsha Freeman*
Books: *Katherine Notley*
Ebooks: *Richard Burden*
Graphics: *Alan Yue*
Photos: *Stuart Lewis*
Circulation Manager: *Stanley Ezrol*

INTELLIGENCE DIRECTORS
Counterintelligence: *Jeffrey Steinberg, Michele Steinberg*
Economics: *John Hoefle, Marcia Merry Baker, Paul Gallagher*
History: *Anton Chaitkin*
Ibero-America: *Dennis Small*
Russia and Eastern Europe: *Rachel Douglas*
United States: *Debra Freeman*

INTERNATIONAL BUREAUS
Bogotá: *Miriam Redondo*
Berlin: *Rainer Apel*
Copenhagen: *Tom Gillesberg*
Houston: *Harley Schlanger*
Lima: *Sara Madueño*
Melbourne: *Robert Barwick*
Mexico City: *Gerardo Castilleja Chávez*
New Delhi: *Ramtanu Maitra*
Paris: *Christine Bierre*
Stockholm: *Ulf Sandmark*
United Nations, N.Y.C.: *Leni Rubinstein*
Washington, D.C.: *William Jones*
Wiesbaden: *Göran Haglund*

ON THE WEB
e-mail: eirns@larouchepub.com
www.larouchepub.com
www.executiveintelligencereview.com
www.larouchepub.com/eiw
Webmaster: *John Sigerson*
Assistant Webmaster: *George Hollis*
Editor, Arabic-language edition: *Hussein Askary*

EIR (ISSN 0273-6314) *is published weekly (50 issues), by EIR News Service, Inc., P.O. Box 17390, Washington, D.C. 20041-0390. (703) 777-9451*

European Headquarters: E.I.R. GmbH, Postfach Bahnstrasse 9a, D-65205, Wiesbaden, Germany Tel: 49-611-73650
Homepage: http://www.eirna.com
e-mail: eirna@eirna.com
Director: Georg Neudecker

Montreal, Canada: 514-461-1557

Denmark: EIR - Danmark, Sankt Knuds Vej 11, basement left, DK-1903 Frederiksberg, Denmark. Tel.: +45 35 43 60 40, Fax: +45 35 43 87 57. e-mail: eirdk@hotmail.com.

Mexico City: EIR, Sor Juana Inés de la Cruz 242-2 Col. Agricultura C.P. 11360 Delegación M. Hidalgo, México D.F. Tel. (5525) 5318-2301
eirmexico@gmail.com

Copyright: ©2015 EIR News Service. All rights reserved. Reproduction in whole or in part without permission strictly prohibited.

Canada Post Publication Sales Agreement #40683579

Postmaster: Send all address changes to *EIR*, P.O. Box 17390, Washington, D.C. 20041-0390.

Signed articles in *EIR* represent the views of the authors, and not necessarily those of the Editorial Board.

Countdown in August

The Short End of a Ride to Extinction

Aug. 3—Lyndon LaRouche insisted on immediate action in the following discussion with the LaRouche PAC Policy Committee today.

We have an interesting situation, he said, in the sense that we're getting closer and closer to doomsday; that is, the point where Obama actually launches thermonuclear war. And it's more and more apparent internationally, that that's the situation that is converging upon civilization right now. And therefore, what we have to do, is actually stop the trend in that direction. We have to get Obama brought under control and removed from the Presidency. Without that mechanism, it's impossible to save civilization, or most of it.

We're in the greatest danger of humanity in the history of the existence of the human species. Therefore, we have to think about what we're going to do to get Obama removed from a controlling position, in terms of the powers of the United States. Without that effect, the probability, the extreme probability, is that there will be an extermination of most of the human population on the planet. Because that's what will happen. It's almost like a kinetic process, where one thing hits the other, one part of the planet hits the other parts of the planet; they interact, they build up, they build up in a combination, and it becomes uncontrollable. And maybe the extinction of the entire human species could occur in this month.

And therefore, the urgency of recognizing this problem, and getting people in positions of power, to *act* upon that evidence! that's what the issue is right now.

Hillary Must Come Forward

It's absolutely necessary that Hillary Clinton come forward now,—not in October but now,—with her direct, first-hand knowledge that Obama ordered her to lie to cover up his criminality in the Benghazi attacks of September 11, 2012.

That's necessary. And it's necessary that it happen quickly. Because to get this thing into motion, you have to have the motion going toward that conclusion soon,—very soon. Things must happen on time, and that means in the present month. And *early* in the present month: *Get this guy out of power!* Without that, the whole human species is in jeopardy right now.

How do you set up a thermonuclear war? Take the case, for example, of the last decade of the Nineteenth Century. That was a gradual buildup, like this one, which became World War I. That process is logical. Now, we're in a very late phase of what is exactly a copy of that process then.

And therefore, it's important not to fool around with things, but to make a large and directed clamor, against anybody who is failing to recognize what the threat is. In other words, any member of Congress, any person of great influence in the United States, who does not recognize *this fact*, should be scurrilously treated for that. Don't let up on them!

Now, you've got a bunch of young people, who are just stupid. Because what we've done, you know, we've bred two generations, or three generations,—you know the recent crop,—and they really are not fit for anything! They have no capability, no sense of responsibility about the human species. They're preoccupied with their own little diddle-diddle, if you know what I mean, and that's what they're preoccupied with.

And so therefore, we have to say that the responsible people, the people who still have minds rather than diddle-diddles,—those people must take charge. This means members of the Congress who are not diddle-

EIR Contents

www.larouchepub.com   Volume 42, Number 31, August 7, 2015

Alan Yue

Cover This Week

Countdown in August

Countdown in August

by My-Hoa Steger

August 3—Were we to act upon the future—to act upon the inherent essence and principle of mankind to grow, develop, and progress,—we could embark upon a new era of a global and galactic renaissance. Were we to continue to disregard this natural principle of man, which qualitatively distinguishes us from the animal species, we will be faced, as we are now, with the threat of a self-inflicted extinction.

As we approach the 70th anniversary of the dropping of the atomic bombs on civilian populations in Hiroshima and Nagasaki on August 6, 1945 and August 9, 1945, respectively, we must unify mankind's intent to say *never again.*

The death of Franklin Delano Roosevelt on April 12, 1945, was a grim turning point in our history. Harry S Truman turned our country away from what FDR had set into motion, and instead launched the era of thermonuclear war. Only under the greatest presidencies since that time, for instance under John F. Kennedy's leadership, were we committed to averting the danger of thermonuclear war.

Today, the future of our species depends on those few who have the courage to confront the reality which stares them dead in the eye. With abundant fact and proof available, from Obama's insistence on building up our nuclear arsenal in Europe, to the resurrection of Right Sector Nazi brigades along Russia's border, we need no more information to verify that, indeed, the future of mankind is in immediate jeopardy.

The CCF: A Project of Bestialization

During Truman's Presidency, a treasonous institution was formed out of West Germany in 1950—the Congress for Cultural Freedom (CCF). The enemy of mankind knows that the conscious power of the human species to transform itself, is the greatest threat to any empire. The Congress for Cultural Freedom was a direct effort to eradicate the knowable and expressible spark of passion in man, which, when acted upon, has the effect of an increase of the potential of our species. The CCF's

mission was to pervert science and culture, to mass-brainwash a population into denying their humanity, and, instead, embracing their bestiality and pessimism.

Two leaders of the CCF's sordid mission were Lord Bertrand Russell and Theodor Adorno. Lord Bertrand Russell was one of the honorary chairmen of the CCF, and was essentially the author of the doctrine of world government through the terror of nuclear weapons. He wrote in his 1951 *The Impact of Science on Society*:

> I think the subject which will be of most importance politically is mass psychology. ... Its importance has been enormously increased by the growth of modern methods of propaganda. Of these the most influential is what is called 'education.' Religion plays a part, though a diminishing one; the press, the cinema, and the radio play an increasing part.

> ... It may be hoped that in time, anybody will be able to persuade anybody of anything if he can catch the patient young, and is provided by the State with money and equipment. The subject will make great strides when it is taken up by scientists under a scientific dictatorship.

> ... The social psychologists of the future will have a number of classes of school children on whom they will try different methods of producing an unshakable conviction that snow is black. Various results will soon be arrived at. First, that the influence of home is obstructive. Second, that not much can be done unless indoctrination begins before the age of ten. Third, that verses set to music and repeatedly intoned are very effective. Fourth, that the opinion that snow is white must be held to show a morbid taste for eccentricity.

> But I anticipate. It is for future scientists to make these maxims precise, and discover exactly how much it costs per head to make children believe that snow is black, and how much

diddle people, and so forth, and people who are serious, must come together and say, 'We are going to prevent this thing from happening." And we have to go out there and force people to come alive. "Don't you realize the threat, that the human species is endangered by this crap? You're going to sit back and say, 'Well, maybe, I don't know; maybe this is not going to happen; maybe it's....'"

But everything is building, step by step, just as from the beginning of the Twentieth Century, from the last decade of the Nineteenth Century, same thing. We're in the same kind of countdown. But this time, it's the big one. And therefore, people who *don't* understand that just should be told, "Hey, jerk? Why're you so damned stupid? Don't you know the human species is in danger, because you and your little, stupid opinions, are blocking the organization of the forces that will stop it?"

We have to lay down the law! We're doing it already. We really have to. The human species is in danger. We have to save the human species. And those who are on the doubter side, well, we'll try to forgive them, as long as we win.

Where to Concentrate

That means that you've got to concentrate on people in the United States, for example, who have the insight and guts, to recognize what the problem is, and to act on the basis of that problem. And therefore, the specter we have is the threat that a bunch of people would say "Well, yes, this is going to happen," and do nothing about it. And that's where the risk comes; the idea that it would be too late, it would be too late for the human species. And that's what the problem is. And that's what has to be stated and addressed. And you have to go hard, against everybody involved in this thing. They've got to do their job, because the existence of the human species is now in jeopardy. And remove this man from power, right now. That would be probably sufficient to stop this thing.

This is something of the greatest possible moment, and it's coming on right now. It's coming within months, within *a* month right now. And that's what the situation is.

And we have a bunch of ignorant people out there, who profess to be ignorant: They don't want to know what's coming down on them, don't want to recognize all the signs, don't want to know the truth. Want to sit there in a cocoon of idiocy. And you have to do something about that, to get people actually sane!

And the problem is that stupidity has become fashionable among the populations of the trans-Atlantic community. That's what it is! The United States, stupidity! The Congress, chiefly represented by stupidity. Most of the institutions, Wall Street, stupidity. People of power, stupidity. And they rely upon the fact that they are in power, and say, "we are in charge," and they're not in charge; they just think they are. And a force which is a real Satanic kind of force is ready to light the fuse and set the whole explosion into motion.

The Stupidity Factor

People do not realize how stupid they are! That is, people who think they are fat-headed and smart and so forth, they don't realize how stupid they are! Just take the case of financial speculation, Wall Street, versus Glass-Steagall, on the other side.

What's the problem? It's that the people of the United States have become stupid. Because what they submit to, is they submit to banking based on a swindle. The banking system is such now, that the banking system is already more than bankrupt, hopelessly bankrupt. The only way we'll get the economy back, assuming we don't go into Hell, is we're going to have to wipe out practically all of Wall Street income. It has to be wiped off. It has no value; it's completely fraudulent.

So what we'll do, the government of the United States must create a new currency process, and use that currency process, under the control of our system of government; and we have to extend the loans, the credit, to get the production going that's needed for mankind. But these questions are not even on the table. And this is the thing we have to cut into.

We need the establishment of a real understanding of what the nature of humanity is. And the knowledge, the actual knowledge of what humanity means, is not understood, or almost not understood by the great majority of the population of the United States in particular, and other parts of the world. They don't understand what humanity is! Because they think of humanity in terms of, "well, you're born, and then you die," and then something else comes up and that's born, and that dies, next. And this kind of monotonous drivel dominates the way that policy is made inside the United States.

"The Harvesters" by Netherlandish Renaissance painter Pieter Bruegel the Elder, in which he depicts the August-September season, c. 1565.

For example, in the Congress: In the Congress in general, that's the standard. There's no sense of reality. There's no sense that there's a threat of the extermination of the human species. When everything is there, on the table, right now, for the extermination of the human species. The weapons of war needed to exterminate the human species, already exist, and are essentially in play, on the edge of being applied. And we do nothing!

Cutting Through the Foolishness

We do nothing. Because we're foolish. And the problem is, how do you cut through the foolishness factor, which dominates the United States? I mean, people are not really intrinsically stupid, but they have become stupid, because they have become *defensive*, and hope that the bad things don't happen to them, when the bad things that are about to happen to them are already coming against them. And they *still* don't understand that they have to fight against this sort of thing, or that they have to combat it in other ways.

And this is where we are. We're at the point of doom, because the end of this month of August, is actu-ally the symbolic, at least, expression of the doom of humanity. Because if the thing goes off, if Obama continues on the project he's been attached to, and continues through the coming weeks into September, we're very close to the extermination of the human species. Why would it happen? Because we paid no attention to reality.

And Hillary is probably one of the targets for extinction by Obama as well. All the conditions about her behavior, suggest she's a disposable personality, therefore, she will be extinguished. Along with the rest of the people. Because that's the character of this man. This man is actually a Satanic figure; which his mother's mate typified in that time, in Asia. And his mother was actually the clone or something, of this mass killer in that part of the world.

We're on a short end of a ride toward extinction of the human species. We don't know exactly how this will go, and so forth, but we know right now, that everything is converging on that, especially the Obama Administration. Obama and the Obama Administration represent Satanic forces, plainly, by the strict definition of Satanic forces, as the destruction of the human species. And by the kinds of methods that are leading toward that kind of destruction. It is Obama essentially; Obama is the one instrument—he's just a chosen instrument; he's a freak.

But anyway, that's the issue: We've got to save humanity; we've got to get humanity to mobilize itself to defend itself, through the vehicle of understanding the *meaning* of the existence of the human species, as opposed to every other living species. When mankind realizes that, that the universe is a desert without mankind,—then that's the time that people begin to understand things.

EIR Contents

www.larouchepub.com Volume 42, Number 31, August 7, 2015

Cover This Week

Countdown in August

Alan Yue

Countdown in August

by My-Hoa Steger

August 3—Were we to act upon the future—to act upon the inherent essence and principle of mankind to grow, develop, and progress,—we could embark upon a new era of a global and galactic renaissance. Were we to continue to disregard this natural principle of man, which qualitatively distinguishes us from the animal species, we will be faced, as we are now, with the threat of a self-inflicted extinction.

As we approach the 70th anniversary of the dropping of the atomic bombs on civilian populations in Hiroshima and Nagasaki on August 6, 1945 and August 9, 1945, respectively, we must unify mankind's intent to say *never again*.

The death of Franklin Delano Roosevelt on April 12, 1945, was a grim turning point in our history. Harry S Truman turned our country away from what FDR had set into motion, and instead launched the era of thermonuclear war. Only under the greatest presidencies since that time, for instance under John F. Kennedy's leadership, were we committed to averting the danger of thermonuclear war.

Today, the future of our species depends on those few who have the courage to confront the reality which stares them dead in the eye. With abundant fact and proof available, from Obama's insistence on building up our nuclear arsenal in Europe, to the resurrection of Right Sector Nazi brigades along Russia's border, we need no more information to verify that, indeed, the future of mankind is in immediate jeopardy.

The CCF: A Project of Bestialization

During Truman's Presidency, a treasonous institution was formed out of West Germany in 1950—the Congress for Cultural Freedom (CCF). The enemy of mankind knows that the conscious power of the human species to transform itself, is the greatest threat to any empire. The Congress for Cultural Freedom was a direct effort to eradicate the knowable and expressible spark of passion in man, which, when acted upon, has the effect of an increase of the potential of our species. The CCF's mission was to pervert science and culture, to mass-brainwash a population into denying their humanity, and, instead, embracing their bestiality and pessimism.

Two leaders of the CCF's sordid mission were Lord Bertrand Russell and Theodor Adorno. Lord Bertrand Russell was one of the honorary chairmen of the CCF, and was essentially the author of the doctrine of world government through the terror of nuclear weapons. He wrote in his 1951 *The Impact of Science on Society*:

> I think the subject which will be of most importance politically is mass psychology. ... Its importance has been enormously increased by the growth of modern methods of propaganda. Of these the most influential is what is called 'education.' Religion plays a part, though a diminishing one; the press, the cinema, and the radio play an increasing part.
>
> ... It may be hoped that in time, anybody will be able to persuade anybody of anything if he can catch the patient young, and is provided by the State with money and equipment. The subject will make great strides when it is taken up by scientists under a scientific dictatorship.
>
> ... The social psychologists of the future will have a number of classes of school children on whom they will try different methods of producing an unshakable conviction that snow is black. Various results will soon be arrived at. First, that the influence of home is obstructive. Second, that not much can be done unless indoctrination begins before the age of ten. Third, that verses set to music and repeatedly intoned are very effective. Fourth, that the opinion that snow is white must be held to show a morbid taste for eccentricity.
>
> But I anticipate. It is for future scientists to make these maxims precise, and discover exactly how much it costs per head to make children believe that snow is black, and how much

Which Mindset Will Lead to Thermonuclear War?

"Modern music sees absolute oblivion as its goal," wrote CCF leader Theodor Adorno.

"Who will drink from the cup?" wrote Lyndon LaRouche in reflecting on mankind's responsibility in 1988. Here, a Fifteenth-century altarpiece of the Passion of Christ, by a northern European artist, and now in the Walters Art Museum in Baltimore, Maryland.

less it would cost to make them believe it is dark gray. Although this science will be diligently studied, it will be rigidly confined to the governing class. The populace will not be allowed to know how its convictions were generated. When the technique has been perfected, every government that has been in charge of education for a generation will be able to control its subjects securely without the need of armies or policemen.

To complement Russell's insane ideology, Theodor Adorno would express his perverted philosophy of music:

What radical music perceives is the untransfigured suffering of man. ... The seismographic registration of traumatic shock becomes, at the same time, the technical structural law of music. It forbids continuity and development. Musical language is polarized according to its extreme: towards gestures of shock resembling bodily convulsions on the one hand, and on the other towards a crystalline standstill of a human being whom anxiety causes to freeze in her tracks...

Modern music sees absolute oblivion as its goal. It is the surviving message of despair from the shipwrecked. It is not that schizophrenia is directly expressed therein; but the music imprints upon itself an attitude similar to that of the mentally ill. The individual brings about his own disintegration. ... He imagines the fulfillment of the promise through magic, but nonetheless within the realm of immediate actuality. ... Its concern is to dominate schizophrenic traits through the aesthetic consciousness. In so doing, it would hope to vindicate insanity as true health.

Who Will Drink the Cup?

To return to the opening point, mankind is faced with the threat of extinction through thermonuclear annihilation. Knowing what we know about the absolute consequences of such actions, should propel us into motion, to say never again. Who are we to take up this mission? Are we merely fleeting organisms of flesh that are born, then die, only to vanish into the dust of the past? It is absolutely imperative that we take up the unified historical mission of those such as Joan of Arc, Johann Sebastian Bach, George Washington, and Lyndon LaRouche, in order to avert the ultimate danger facing mankind.

The weight and magnitude of our present day's choice reminds this author of an excerpt of Mr. LaRouche's writing, written in March 1988, essentially on the eve of entering prison, after having been targeted by the likes of George Bush, Sr. and Henry Kissinger, and marked for political and personal assassination:

Up to a critical point in our lives, we plod our craft and pursue our moral commitments honestly to the limit of our knowledge and strength of will to do so. In that respect, we are all ordinary. Then, one day, to some among us ordinary folk, there comes an experience which we must fairly liken to the New Testament's account of Christ in Gethsemane. It is not enough to propose, to foster, to support those causes we know to be good. A silent voice speaks to us: If there is no one else to lead, you must do so. We protest: "Who am I, and what my poor means to undertake such a mission? Can there not be leaders which I can support, and so fulfill the responsibility in a manner consistent with my pitiable means?"

Then, in a moment permeated with a special quality of terror, we know that we drink from that cup. What do most ordinary folk, of the sort we were a moment earlier, know of such terror? To know such terror, one must first love mankind, and love truth. One must see mankind as doomed to some horrible consequence, unless a great change is made. The terror is the perception that this necessary change will not occur, unless one oneself acts appropriately to bring it

about against all odds. As one drinks from that cup, there is a transformation in the nature of one's will, and a congruent transformation in one's state of knowledge.

'Es Ist Vollbracht'

Our culture is the expression of our inner soul. It is the fundamental concept which drives and shapes our strategic thought and policies. This is why many of the discussions between Mr. LaRouche and our extended organization have repeatedly emphasized the musical principle of placement. Not of the note, but placement of the tone—of the mind. For much of its history, mankind has suffered under the tyranny of mathematical deduction, of literal interpretation and description, rather than having access to subtle insights into true beauty.

In confronting today's horrors, most people want quick solutions, quick fixes, like a heroine addict—answer the question and get it over with; shoot me up and let me forget about reality! If we are to be victorious in this war of the Divine Good over Satanic Evil, we must have the courage to delve deeper, and act upon the principles of the human spirit.

To provide our readers with an example of such a bold spirit, we look to J.S. Bach, and the subject matter he takes up in composing the story of the *St. John Passion*. Representative of the inherent intention of mankind to look forward, into the future, is Bach's "Es ist vollbracht" alto aria from that composition.

The question of placement is not in the mere sung notes of the composition. The music does not come from the aggregation of notes in a literal sequence, dictated from history by the composer. What dictates to us the placement of tone? What is it inside us, that dictates the unfolding of a profound idea? What are we subject to in the hands of these great minds of the past? We are subject to just what they are subject to—a passion for mankind, past, present, and future. An accountability to hold these works as sacred and spiritual, and to submit ourselves to the mission to ensure that future generations have access, and are given the opportunity, to transcend these beautiful, universal ideas.

Thermonuclear war would surely end that mission of mankind, once and for all.

Let us take with us Bach's image of the Passion of Christ, as told in the Gospel of John in this special moment of ambiguity, where the future remains to be shaped, to be created. Nothing is inevitable and nothing is predetermined. The beautiful and good can, and must, prevail.

Es Ist Vollbracht

Es ist vollbracht!
O Trost vor die gekränkten Seelen!
Die Trauernacht
Läßt nun die letzte Stunde zählen.
Der Held aus Juda siegt mit Macht
Und schließt den Kampf.
Es ist vollbracht!

It is accomplished!
O comfort for the ailing soul!
The night of sorrow
Now measures out its last hour.
The hero out of Judah conquers with might
And concludes the battle.
It is accomplished!

A performance of this aria by a soloist from the Tölzer Knabenchor can be seen here.

How Eisenhower Stopped Truman's March to Nuclear Armageddon

by Dean Andromidas

Aug. 2—It is a safe historical assessment that the election of General Dwight D. Eisenhower to the Presidency of the United States in November 1952 stopped the march to nuclear Armageddon put into motion by President Harry S Truman. In November 1952, two days before the election, in an apparent effort to boost the sagging campaign of Truman's chosen successor, the hapless Adlai Stevenson, the lame duck President Truman ordered the testing of America's first hydrogen bomb.

Perhaps that test, in the midst of the ongoing war without end on the Korean Peninsula, gave Eisenhower the added boost to win one of the most impressive presidential elections victories in the history of the United States.

This report will endeavor to demonstrate how Eisenhower, in the first year of his administration, acted decisively, and with great dispatch, to end the danger of universal war. The best way to begin is with the very end of the story, the last speech of his Presidency, the famous speech warning the American people of the dangers of the military-industrial complex. It is remarkable for an outgoing President to warn his fellow citizens of a danger from within, not from "subversive communism," as one would expect during the height of the so-called Cold War, but from his country's own military-political-security establishment, of which he himself had been a part for his entire professional career. It is probably one of the most important speeches of the Twentieth Century.

Let's look a little more closely at what he said:

...we must guard against the acquisition of unwarranted influence, whether sought or unsought, by the military-industrial complex. The potential for the *disastrous rise of misplaced power exists and will persist. We must never let the weight of this combination endanger our liberties or democratic processes. We should take nothing for granted...* (emphasis added).

These heavy words from an outgoing President were unprecedented. Equally important is the second point he made in the speech where he refers to the scientific research establishment:

The prospect of domination of the nation's scholars by Federal employment, project allocations, and the *power of money is ever present and is gravely to be regarded.* Yet, in holding scientific research and discovery in respect, as we should, we must also be alert to the equal and

President Eisenhower delivered a shock with his farewell address on January 17, 1961.

en.wikipedia.org

opposite *danger that public policy could itself become the captive of a scientific technological elite...* (emphasis added)

Eisenhower is obviously not talking about the Einsteins or Oppenheimers, but institutions like the RAND Corporation, the Ford Foundation, and all the others that make public policy through private financial interests. American statesman Lyndon H. LaRouche has been warning about this danger for the last four decades.

As President, Eisenhower was constantly fighting on three fronts. First, there was the Soviet Union, which was problematic in those days; then came the British Empire, whose imperial designs he had to fight while at the same time trying to build an alliance with the nation of Great Britain. And then, behind his own lines, he was always battling this military-industrial complex, which he obviously saw as the most dangerous of all.

Eisenhower conducted this war without having to actually use the massive military power the United States possessed. Rather than using the principle of brute force, he acted upon another principle, a much higher principle, which he found in the history and traditions of his own country, as he understood them. He also states this principle in this same speech:

"It is the task of *statesmanship* to mold, to balance, and to integrate these and other forces, new and old, within the principles of our democratic system — ever aiming toward the supreme goals of our free society..." (emphasis added).

Truman's March to Nuclear Armageddon

Within weeks of the death of President Franklin D Roosevelt in April of 1945, Truman launched his march to a nuclear World War III, when he ordered the dropping of two atomic bombs on Japan, an adversary that had lost all hope of prosecuting the war, and was about to surrender to the United States. It was an obvious act of terror aimed against the Soviet Union and the world through the mass murder of a virtually defenseless population.

When briefed on Truman's intention to drop atomic bombs on Japan in July 1945 by then Secretary of War Henry Stimson, Eisenhower recalled in his memoirs:

During his recitation of the relevant facts, I had been conscious of a feeling of depression and so I voiced to him my grave misgivings, first on the basis of my belief that Japan was already defeated and that dropping the bomb was completely unnecessary, and secondly because I thought that our country should avoid shocking world opinion by the use of a weapon whose employment was, I thought, no longer mandatory as a measure to save lives. It was my belief that Japan was at that very moment, seeking some way to surrender with a minimum loss of 'face.' The Secretary was deeply perturbed by my attitude, almost angrily refuting the reasons I gave for my quick conclusions.

Eisenhower was not the only senior military officer to have denounced the use of the bomb. Admiral William D. Leahy, who had been Roosevelt's chief military advisor, also opposed the use of the bomb. Although he served Truman loyally until 1949, nonetheless Leahy wrote the following in his memoirs, published in 1950:

It is my opinion that the use of this barbarous weapon at Hiroshima and Nagasaki was of no material assistance in our war against Japan. The Japanese were already defeated and ready to surrender.... My own feeling was that in being the first to use it, we had adopted the ethical standard common to the barbarians of the Dark Ages. I was not taught to make war in that fashion, and wars cannot be won by destroying women and children.

MacArthur also opposed use of the bomb. According to Richard Nixon,

MacArthur once spoke to me very eloquently about it... He thought it a tragedy that the bomb was ever exploded. MacArthur believed that the same restrictions ought to apply to atomic weapons as to conventional weapons, the military objective should always be to limit damage to non combatants... MacArthur, you see, was a soldier. He believed in using force only against military targets, and that is why the nuclear thing turned him off, which I think speaks well of him.

Joining them in their opposition would be such war heroes as Five Star Admiral William "Bull" Halsey, Admiral Lewis L. Strauss, who had been deeply involved in the atomic bomb project, and was later named by Eisenhower to the chairmanship of the Atomic Energy Commission, and many other leading scientists.

Truman did not listen to these warnings, and he was backed by others who would later become part of the "military-industrial complex."

The bombs were dropped, the slaughter exposed to the entire world, and Generalissimo Joseph Stalin ordered work on the Soviet Union's first atomic bomb to be accelerated. The wartime alliance that defeated fascism received its first, if not fatal blow.

If the intention of dropping the bombs on Japan was to somehow win support among the American population for this new doctrine of mass murder, it was not very successful. America was war-wary, memories of their "gallant allies," the Soviet Union, were still fresh in the collective conscience, and there were still many pro-Roosevelt New Dealers in government and the military. Therefore Truman's first Administration had to confine itself to creating the so-called Cold War, while his second would plot nuclear war.

To kick off his "Cold War," Truman, in March 1946, within seven months of the end of the war, invited Winston Churchill, then out of government, to Fulton, Missouri, Truman's home state, to deliver his infamous Iron Curtain speech. Churchill called for Russia to take down the "Iron Curtain" it had allegedly created across Europe and join a "World Government" he was proposing, that would guarantee peace through a nuclear arsenal controlled by the "Special Relationship" between the British Empire and the United States.

The evil Bertrand "Dirty Bertie" Russell completed the doctrine in his infamous article that appeared in the same year in the United States Bulletin of Atomic Scientists, where he called on the Soviets to join the World Government or face preemptive atomic war.

"...If Russia acquiesced willingly, all would be well, If not, it would be necessary to bring pressure to

EIRNS/Stuart Lewis

Principal author of the "Cold War Plan," NSC-68, former investment banker turned State Department official, Paul Nitze. Here he appears at the National Press Club in 1987.

bear, even to the extent of risking war... If Russia does not agree to join, there will be war sooner or later...," warned Russell.

Not only did Stalin refuse, but American public opinion was decidedly turned off by Churchill's ravings. Nonetheless, the Cold War set in, with Truman making no effort whatsoever to even talk to Stalin. In fact, Truman said he would meet the Soviet leader only if Stalin came to the United States, which, of course, everyone knew Stalin would not do, for security reasons.

By Truman's second term, the Cold War was at its height, and in August 1949 Russia tested its first atomic bomb and was soon on the road to developing a thermonuclear, hydrogen bomb.

With many of the New Dealers and moderates having left government in disgust, a new breed of policy-maker marched into the Administration, opening the way to launch a preventive war doctrine. The representatives of the military-industrial complex marched into the new administration. Among the most noteworthy was the evil Paul Nitze, a former investment banker and commodity speculator with the private bank, Dillon Reed.

From his perch on the Policy Planning Staff in the State Department, Nitze was among those calling for an "appropriate response" to the Soviets' testing of a nuclear bomb. That response would be to declare the United States at war with the Soviet Union, which now required a massive military build-up, which in fact increased the defense budget by more than 400 percent.

This undeclared, declaration of war was embodied in the National Security Council Directive NSC-68: "United States Objectives and Programs for National Security," completed on April 14, 1950. Nitze was the principal author of this document. It was the "Cold War Plan." Like an H.G. Wells science fiction novel, one section read: Motivated by a "fanatical faith... the fundamental Design of the Kremlin" is to destroy the United States "as the center of power in the non-Soviet world... whose integrity and vitality must be subverted or destroyed by one means or another if the Kremlin is to achieve its fundamental design."

NSC-68 asserted that a massive military build-up had to be completed by 1954, because that was the date, it was claimed, of "maximum danger," since by that time the Soviet Union would have enough atomic bombs to launch a first strike against the United States.

> The execution of such a build-up, however, requires that the United State have an affirmative program beyond the solely defensive one of countering the threat posed by the Soviet Union.... it must envisage the political and economic measures with which, and the military shield behind which, the free world can work to frustrate the Kremlin Design by the strategy of the cold war...The whole success of the proposed program hangs ultimately on recognition by this Government, the American people, and all free peoples, that the *cold war is in fact a real war in which the survival of the free world is at stake* (emphasis added).

This new doctrine demanded that the United States must always maintain absolute military superiority over Russia, including having more strategic bombers, more missiles and above all, more nuclear weapons. Such a doctrine was militarily incompetent, since deterrence does not depend on absolute military superiority: such doctrines actually are the cause of wars. What followed was an orgy of immensely wasteful spending that created mountains of actually obsolete military systems such as the B-36 bomber, which was already obsolete on the drawing board, but which lined the pockets of those whom Eisenhower warned against.

When one declares war, one should not be surprised if a war begins. The adoption of this new doctrine in April of 1950, had an almost immediate effect. On June 25, 1950 North Korean troops began storming across the 38th parallel, thus beginning the Korean war.

Despite the fact that General Douglas MacArthur had virtually won the war with his attack on Inchon, and subsequent routing of the North Korean army back across the 38th parallel, Truman did nothing to seek a diplomatic end to the war. When China intervened, MacArthur was ordered not to bomb the bridges over the Yalu river, on the claim that the action would create a bigger war, and it was "the wrong war in the wrong place," begging the question of what was the "right war and right place."[1]

MacArthur was dismissed, and the war became a killing field like the Vietnam War. The Defense budget went from 10 billion to over 40 billion dollars as the military buildup accelerated the massive production of nuclear bombs and bombers and missiles, and aircraft carriers to deliver them. The build-up would continue to prepare for the year of "maximum danger," 1954 when the "right war in the right place" might present itself.

Eisenhower Decides He Must Save the Nation, Seeks the Presidency

Eisenhower was never one of Truman's "team players," Quite the contrary. He grew to detest the Kansas city haberdasher-turned-president for his pettiness, incompetence, and dangerous foreign policy, where Truman allowed the British to lead him by the nose to help them save their crumbling empire. By 1948, after a term as Chief of Staff of the Army, Eisenhower went into unofficial retirement from the military, and took the position of president of Columbia University in New York City.

[Note: As one of the handful of Five Star Generals named in World War II, Eisenhower would always be on the active list. Nonetheless, when he became president, he resigned his commission.]

Despite popular demand for him to run for the 1948 presidential campaign by millions of Americans, especially war veterans, including the sons of Franklin D. Roosevelt and the young Lyndon H LaRouche, Eisenhower remained at Columbia.

If he had become President in 1948, the world would have been a very, very different place than we have today, because Eisenhower had a very clear conception of America's place in the post-war world. In many respects it was very similar to that of FDR. While at Columbia, he worked through these conceptions. Like FDR, he saw that the United States, as the world's leading Republic and most powerful economy, must play its historic leading role. The task was clear: maintain world peace through the institution of the United Nations, as conceived by FDR, restore the trust between the United States and Russia that promised a new world order of

---

1. See "MacArthur's Victory at Inchon: Defeating the British Empire," by Don Phau and Dean Andromidas, *EIR*, April 12, 2013.

peace and cooperation at the end of the war, and begin the process of dismantling the European Empires of France, the Netherlands, and above all, the British.

His view of the Soviet Union at the end of World War II, and in 1948, was expressed in his Wartime memoir, *Crusade in Europe*, published in 1948. There he described his visit to Moscow in August 1945, when he talked with Stalin, while attending a sports parade.

He [Stalin] evinced great interest in the industrial, scientific, educational and social achievements of America. He repeated several times that it was necessary for Russia to remain friends with the United States. Speaking through an interpreter, he said in effect: 'There are many ways in which we need American help. It is our great task to raise the standards of living of the Russian people, which have been seriously damaged by the war. We must learn all about your scientific achievements in agriculture. Likewise, we must get your technicians to help us in our engineering and construction problems, and we want to know more about mass production methods in factories. We know that we are behind in these things and we know that you can help us.' This general trend of thought he pursued in many directions, whereas I had supposed that he would content himself merely with some expression of desire to cooperate.

Putting the desire to cooperate in a broader context, Eisenhower wrote:

In the past relations of America and Russia there was no cause to regard the future with pessimism. Historically, the two peoples had maintained an unbroken friendship that dated back to the birth of the United States as an independent republic. Except for a short period, their diplomatic relations had been continuous. Both were free from the stigma of colonial empire-building by force. The transfer between them of the rich Alaskan territory was an unmatched international episode, devoid of threat at the time and of any rumination after the exchange. Twice they had been allies in war. Since 1941 they had been

Evgeni Khaldeï

General Eisenhower and Marshall Zhukov at ceremonies in Moscow, August 1945. During the visit, Eisenhower expressed optimism about restoring the "unbroken friendship which dated back to the birth of the United States as an independent republic."

dependent each on the other for ultimate victory over the European Axis.

After reviewing the obvious differences and potential for conflict between the two powers, Eisenhower continued: "Should the gulf, however, be bridged practically by effective methods of cooperation, the peace and unity of the world would be assured. No other division among nations could be considered a menace to world unity and peace, provided mutual confidence and trust could be developed between America and the Soviets."

At the outbreak of the Korean war in 1950, Truman requested that Eisenhower return to active duty to establish the military command of NATO, the Supreme Allied Headquarters in France. Establishing the headquarters and building an allied command was a task Eisenhower put his heart into, and used it to help create a new military doctrine he would implement as President.

Eisenhower was in France when he heard that Truman had fired General Douglas MacArthur from command in Korea, for the crime of wanting to terminate the war as soon as possible. It was from Europe that he saw Korea become a quagmire because the Truman Administration refused to end it, and it was in 1952 when he read that Truman intended to increase the defense budget from $40-65 billion. That same year, while still in Europe, Eisenhower decided to run for the Republican Presidential nomination.

Eisenhower knew what his mission as president was: reverse the march to Armageddon, launched by Truman, beginning with ending the Korean war; reversing the preventive war doctrine initiated by NSC-68, bringing the United States strategic doctrine to that of true deterrence which would enable the reduction and stabilization of the defense budget, and endeavoring to reestablish the wartime trust between the U.S and Russia.

Popular history attacks Eisenhower for his so-called doctrine of "massive retaliation" with nuclear weapons. While nuclear weapons in fact played a central role in the doctrine, the emphasis was on "retaliation," not preemption. Nor did it include what became, after the assassination of President John F. Kennedy, the dangerous doctrine of so-called "flexible response," which was to carry out proxy wars, even in the middle of Europe and maintain them below the nuclear threshold, a very dangerous and impossible-to-control doctrine.

A deterrent doctrine did not require absolute military superiority, especially with nuclear weapons. You can only destroy the world once. Eisenhower had a conception of mobile military forces that would allow rapid deployment for concentration at chosen points in case of emergency. It was a doctrine that would enable the reduction of military forces. This became the so-called "New Look" doctrine. Since Eisenhower opposed any type of colonial or proxy wars, a super-large standing military force was not required. Indeed, under Eisenhower, the United States did not engage in any colonial war.

End the Korean War by Ending the Cold War

The major plank of Eisenhower's presidential campaign was to end the bloodbath in Korea, and recalibrate United States defense doctrine to one of true deterrence. He promised the electorate that he would visit Korea on an inspection trip as soon as he was elected, even before his inauguration, a promise he kept.

Eisenhower had a secret, or not-so-secret, weapon not only to end Korean War, but to reestablish trust between the United States and the Soviet Union. That secret weapon was his old commander and war time collaborator, General Douglas MacArthur, for whom Eisenhower served as chief deputy for almost ten years

President-elect Dwight D. Eisenhower (left) during his visit to Korea in December 1952.

in the 1930s, when MacArthur was Chief of Staff of the Army, and later chief military advisor to the Philippines. It is a story fully elaborated in the *EIR article*, "Eisenhower's Fight Against the British Empire's Cold War" by this author. [2] We can only summarize it here.

As promised, Eisenhower conducted an inspection of the Korean war front within days of his election victory. Upon his return he held a meeting with MacArthur on December 17, 1952 where he was presented with a memorandum calling for ending the Korean War through coming to a series of understandings with Stalin that would resolve all major points of conflict between the Soviet Union and the United States and its European Allies. This would require a series of summit meetings between Eisenhower and Stalin, without any third country involvement; especially without the involvement of the British and their prime minister, Winston Churchill.

The United States would propose not only the

---

2. Dean Andromidas, "Eisenhower's Fight Against the British Empire's 'Cold War.'" *EIR*, September 24, 2010.

ending of the Korean War, but putting an end to the division of Germany. Both countries would be allowed to unite under forms of popularly determined governments, and, along with Austria and Japan, all four countries would become neutral under guarantee of the United States and the USSR.

With Stalin and Eisenhower once again sitting at the same table, as during the summits of World War II, the Cold War would be virtually over.

As documented in the above-mentioned article, Eisenhower fully embraced this plan, and diplomatic moves were made for an Eisenhower-Stalin Summit. Of course, Churchill was horrified as being the third man out, watching the potential for an American-Russian Alliance, which for 200 years the British Empire had endeavored to prevent. Nonetheless, the idea of these two iconic wartime leaders holding a summit electrified popular opinion in the United States.

Following the inauguration, Eisenhower named State department Russian expert, Chip Bohlen, who had served as FDR's interpreter during all of the latter's meetings with Stalin, as the new ambassador to Moscow. Alas, on March 5, 1953, in the midst of preliminaries for the summit, Stalin died, and this unique opportunity to end the East-West divide died in stillbirth. A new, untested, and unsure leadership came forward in Moscow, that precluded any new and bold initiatives on both sides.

In April, Eisenhower presented his "Chance of Peace" speech as an effort to sound out the new leaders. In that speech he specifically called for completing the negotiations to end the Korean war, and the negotiations for an Austrian peace treaty that would see the withdrawal of all foreign troops and the neutralization of the country guaranteed by all the major powers. Not unexpectedly, there was no positive response from the Soviet side.

Nonetheless the Korean Armistice was signed on July 27, 1953. The Austrian peace treaty and subsequent removal of all foreign troops and its neutralization did not occur until May 15, 1955.

The New York Times' *Christmas Day 1952 interview with Josef Stalin, in which Stalin welcomes the idea of a meeting with Eisenhower. The British were apoplectic.*

Solarium Project: Deconstructing the Preventive War Doctrine

Denied the political and positive strategic momentum that a Stalin-Eisenhower summit would generate, Eisenhower was faced with dismantling the "Cold War plan" and provocative doctrine that permeated the American security-military institutions and establishment in Washington, even in his own Administration. Very specifically, he had to reverse the provocative NSC-68 policy. This was done in typical Eisenhower fashion. He would force his entire security staff through an exercise that would make perfectly clear the failures and dangers of NSC-68, in contrast to what his policy would be.

During a meeting with some of his top advisors in the White House solarium, he came up with the idea of the Solarium Project. The project would serve to thrash out the three major strategic doctrines that were being bandied about at that time, especially in NSC-68; in reality, refute them; and in doing this in the presence of Eisenhower's entire security establishment, expound his own, contrary policy.

Many years later, General Andrew J. Goodpaster, who served as one of Eisenhower's closest and trusted White House advisors, commented on the President's purpose for the project.

It was quite characteristic of his way of doing business. He wanted to get… all the responsible people in the room, [have them] take up the issues and hear their views. He had what amounted to a tacit rule that there could be no nonconcurrence through silence. If somebody didn't agree, he was obliged to speak his mind and get it all out on the table or [directly to him] in the Oval office. And then in light of all that, the president would come to a line of action. He wanted everybody to participate in it. And then he wanted everybody to be guided by it.[3]

The project established three groups of experts who would study the three doctrines embodied in NSC-68. This included the so-called containment policy first enunciated by State Department Russia expert George Kennan, who also participated. The latter, despite being a died-in-the-wool anti-Soviet policy maker, who thought it would be impossible to come to serious agreements with the Soviet regime, had in fact left the State Department in 1950 because under NSC-68 and Nitze, containment had been militarized and could lead to war.

The second doctrine was the "line in the sand" policy, where literally a line would be drawn on the map such that, if the Soviets crossed it, war would become inevitable.

The third was the so-called "roll back," using methods short of war to roll back Soviet influence until it presumably collapsed.

Eisenhower had designed this exercise to have, for the first time, teams of very high level experts work intensely for six weeks to elaborate fully these doctrines. Eisenhower included certain of his own more trusted experts, such as General Goodpaster, who participated in the roll-back team, to assure thoroughness that would demonstrate the dangers and positive concepts, if any, implied in all three, especially the "line in the sand" and "roll back" and "date of maximum danger" as stated in NSC-68.

At the end of their deliberations, the teams presented their findings before a forum held in the White House basement attended by the administration's entire security establishment, including the Joint Chiefs of Staff, the National Security Council Staff, etc., in all some 70 people.

At the end of these presentations, Eisenhower presented his own summary and conclusions. He prefaced those remarks with the statement, "The only thing worse than losing a nuclear war, is winning a nuclear war." He then proceeded to expound upon what he saw as valid and as dangers in each of the doctrines. While a transcript of his comments is not available, Goodpaster commented, Eisenhower "wanted to reduce the militarization of the United States-Soviet Cold War confrontation."[4]

Revoking the Preventive War Doctrine

The end result of the project, in June 1953, was the drafting of NSC 162/2 which virtually reversed the most dangerous parts of NSC-68. Many observers see it as a banning of preventive war. By no means is the document a peace manifesto, and it pulled no punches on what it saw as clear Soviet threats. Nonetheless, it reads much differently than the NSC-68. Gone is the idea of the "date of maximum danger." In fact, it states, "The USSR does not seem likely deliberately to launch a general war against the United States during the period covered by current estimates...." In fact, it states that it is "improbable." The document warns against western actions that the Soviets "may view as a serious threat to their security" because the Soviets would not be "deterred by fear of general war from taking the measures necessary to counter" these actions.

The document further states that while the United States must improve its strength in the face of a Soviet threat, it, "must also keep open the possibility of negotiating with the USSR and Communist China acceptable and enforceable agreements...." While the policy of the United States is to prevent Soviet aggression, [it is also] to establish an effective control of armaments under proper safeguards, but is not to dictate the internal political and economic organization of the USSR."

Much of the document refers to building and strengthening the western alliance, recognizing that, since the countries of Europe hope for the creation of a durable peace, therefore the U.S. must dispel their fears that the U.S. policy holds risks "ranging from preventive war and liberation, to withdrawal into isolation." Therefore the US must " seek to convince them of its

---

3. *George F. Kennan and the Origins of Eisenhower's New Look: An Oral History of Project Solarium,* William B. Pickett, editor, Princeton Institute for International and Regional Studies, Monograph Series Number 1, Princeton University, 2004.

---

4. *Ibid.*

UN photo/MB

President Eisenhower delivers his Atoms for Peace proposal to the United Nations on December 8, 1953.

developed his own plan which would be enunciated in an address before the General Assembly of the United Nations on December 8, 1953.

This was the Atoms for Peace plan, which presaged Lyndon La-Rouche's 1970's conception of the Strategic Defense Initiative,—that is, called for establishing a mission, where both the United States and Soviet Union could cooperate on a program that could deploy their immense scientific capacities away from developing weapons for mutual mass destruction, toward benefitting all of humanity.

As Eisenhower said:

For me to say that the defense capabilities of the United States are such that they could inflict terrible losses upon an aggressor—for me to say that the retaliation capabilities of the United States are so great that such an aggressor's land would be laid waste—all this, while fact, is not the true expression of the purpose and the hope of the United States.

To pause there would be to confirm the hopeless finality of a belief that two atomic colossi are doomed malevolently to eye each other indefinitely across a trembling world. To stop there would be to accept helplessly the probability of civilization destroyed—the annihilation of the irreplaceable heritage of mankind handed down to us generation from generation—and the condemnation of mankind to begin all over again the age-old struggle upward from savagery toward decency, and right, and justice.

Surely no sane member of the human race could discover victory in such desolation. Could anyone wish his name to be coupled by history with such human degradation and destruction....

So my country's purpose is to help us move out of the dark chamber of horrors into the light, to find a way by which the minds of men, the hopes of men, the souls of men everywhere, can

desire to reach such settlements" with the Soviet Union.

Rather than positing a call for a huge military build-up, it calls on the U.S. to maintain the required military strength required to counter the Soviet threat, but "at the least feasible cost."

Atoms for Peace

While NSC 162/2 put an end to the preventive war doctrine of the Truman administration, it was not a positive policy that would put the world on the road towards putting an end to the causes that underlay the danger of nuclear Armageddon.

Working with his closest advisors, Eisenhower put forward various initiatives, including a grand settlement of the division of Europe calling for the reunification of Germany and the withdrawal U.S. and Russian troops from Western and Eastern Europe. While this was deemed impractical because of not only the unsettled leadership transition in the Soviet Union but also opposition within Western Europe itself, Eisenhower move forward toward peace and happiness and wellbeing.

The proposal was simple and straightforward. To establish an Atomic Energy Agency where those "principally involved" nations, which must include the Soviet Union, would contribute to the establishment of a bank of fissionable material that would be made available to all the nations of the United Nations "to serve the peaceful pursuits of mankind. Experts would be mobilized to apply atomic energy to the needs of agriculture, medicine, and other peaceful activities. A special purpose would be to provide abundant electrical energy in the power-starved areas of the world. Thus the contributing powers would be dedicating some of their strength to serve the needs rather than the fears of mankind."

This would "allow all peoples of all nations to see that, in this enlightened age, the great powers of the earth, both of the East and of the West, are interested in human aspirations first, rather than in building up the armaments of war...."

Furthermore, it would "open up a new channel for peaceful discussion," both private and public, to make progress in advances toward peace "to find the way by which the miraculous inventiveness of man shall not be dedicated to his death, but consecrated to his life."

Not only did the Soviet Union accept the challenge, but with the establishment of the International Atomic Energy Commission, the science of nuclear power was no longer confined to weapons laboratories operating under top secrecy, but became available for the whole world, thus opening the potential for establishing an entirely new scientific and technological platform for the world economy.

These were the accomplishments of Eisenhower in the first year of his Administration. As anyone can see,

creative commons/Fleet Air Army

This photograph from the British Imperial War Museum collection, shows smoke rising from the oil tanks beside the Suez Canal, which had been hit during the initial Anglo-French assault on Port Said, November 5, 1956.

it was a dramatic shift from the Truman Administration's "chamber of horrors," to the potential for change and cooperation.

The Empire Strikes Back

Of course, the fight did not end there. In fact, it only was the beginning. The British Empire and the military-industrial complex fought back against Eisenhower's determination to bring American policy back to the traditions of seeking peace and economic progress. This article will not elucidate that fight but will make a brief comment on it.

From the very moment he was elected President, Eisenhower came into conflict with the British Empire and its major advocate, Prime Minister Winston Churchill, who desparately worked to save the crumbling British Empire. The conflict expressed itself over Churchill's determination that the British hegemony over the Middle East should be fully protected, especially maintaining control of the Suez Canal and the huge military base, the largest in the world, that encompassed the entire Canal Zone and where no less than 80,000 British troops were stationed in 1953.

Churchill's "Eighteenth Century" world outlook was a total antithesis of Eisenhower's. Like Roosevelt, Eisenhower believed colonial empires should be dismantled, and new nations created and supported in their struggle for economic development. These two world views came into conflict over Egypt, generating serious tension between the United States and Britain from the very beginning of the Eisenhower Administrations. That conflict is well documented.

Eisenhower saw no need for Great Britain, which was always teetering on the edge of bankruptcy since the end of World War II, to maintain the extravagance of having 80,000 troops in Egypt, an independent nation. It was clear to Eisenhower that those troops were there not to protect the canal zone from Soviet aggression, since everyone knew Russia had neither the capability nor the intention of attacking the Canal. They were there to reinforce the Empire's domination of the entire region.

Eisenhower actually admired President Gamal Abdel Nasser as a dynamic nationalist leader seeking to assert his country's independence and leadership role in the Middle East and Africa. Eisenhower held a similar admiration for India's Prime Minister Jawaharlal Nehru.

Under United States persuasion and pressure, Britain withdrew its troops in 1954. In the same year Eisenhower wrote Churchill calling on him to take an initiative that would immortalize him as a world historic figure by announcing the dismantling of the British Empire! In the July 22 letter Eisenhower said, "Colonialism is on its way out as a relationship among peoples:.." The letter suggested that Churchill give a speech calling for the establishment of a program, funded by the leading western powers, to express sympathy, and support educational and economic programs, and political development among the nations, and colonies of Africa, Asia, South America, etc. He goes on:

> Possibly it might be said that our nations plan to undertake every kind of applicable program to insure that within a space of twenty-five years, all peoples will have achieved the necessary political, cultural and economic standards to permit the attainment of their goals.
>
> If you could say that twenty-five years from now, every last one of the colonies (excepting military bases) should have been offered a right

to self-government and determination, you would electrify the world. . . .

Churchill was not amused. In response, he admitted he was a "laggard" when it came to offering independence to Britain's colonies, but added, "I am a bit skeptical about universal suffrage for the Hottentots. . . ." He reasserted his belief in "the unity of the English speaking peoples" and the "special relationship" between the United States and the British Empire.

This basic conflict exploded on the world stage in October 1956, when Churchill's successor, Anthony Eden, in cahoots with the French and Israelis, and without informing Eisenhower, invaded Egypt to seize the Suez Canal. which had been nationalized, within Egypt's legal rights under the Canal treaty and international law. Occurring on October 29, only a few days before the presidential elections, the action was also calculated to undermine Eisenhower's bid for re-election.

Eisenhower was enraged by the British double cross, but was not surprised. He acted with dispatch, taking the issue to the United Nations, imposing unprecedented pressure on Britain, including by supporting a run on the pound and blocking a desperately needed International Monetary Fund loan to Britain. He forced the withdrawal of British, French, and Israeli forces from Egypt. Under the cover of a nervous breakdown, Eden resigned as prime minister to appease the enraged Eisenhower.

Parallel to the Suez Crisis was the Hungarian revolution of 1956, which culminated with the Soviet invasion of that country on November 2. Many have observed that the Soviets' decision to invade was prompted by the attack on Egypt. The two crises could have rapidly escalated into a superpower confrontation, and even nuclear war. The revolt itself came at a time when discussions over the situation in Eastern Europe between the Soviets and the Eisenhower administration were underway.

Seeing the dangers, Eisenhower sought to de-escalate the situation, and confined his action to appropriate UN resolutions and extension of humanitarian aid and denunciation of the invasion. Reflecting on his decision not to intervene militarily, Eisenhower wrote in his memoirs: "Sending United States troops alone into Hungary through hostile or neutral territory would have involved us in general war. . . . [I]t was obvious that no mandate for military action could or would be forth-

National Archives

"I hate war as only a soldier who has lived it can, only as one who has seen its brutality, its stupidity," said General Dwight Eisenhower in 1946. Here, he talks with the troops just prior to the D-Day invasion, June 6, 1944.

coming. I realized that there was no use going further into this possibility."

As for the elections, Eisenhower declared the break with the "special relationship" over Suez was the United States' "second Declaration of Independence" in foreign policy. Eisenhower won an even more impressive electoral victory than in 1952. Nonetheless, the Republicans lost their majority in both houses of Congress.

One should not forget Eisenhower's policy toward France. He absolutely refused any U.S. military intervention whatsoever, to bailout the French after their spectacular defeat in Dien Bien Phu in Indochina.[5]

The Military-industrial Complex Strikes back

Eisenhower's crushing of the British imperialist intervention, did not stop the military-industrial complex from fighting back. The most dramatic example of their attack on Eisenhower was the so-called Gaither report, which was nothing less than a reincarnation of NSC-68. It was leaked to the *New York Times* in the wake of the

---

5. In fact, warhawks in Eisenhower's own Joint Chiefs of Staff, with the backet of Secretary of State John Foster Dulles, went so far as to advocate U.S. pre-emptive use of nuclear weapons in defense of the French effort to hold on to Indo-China. Eisenhower adamantly refused, saying: "You boys must be crazy. We can't use those awful weapons against Asians for the second time in ten years. My God."

Soviet launching of Sputnik in 1957.

On October 4, 1957, the Soviets launched Sputnik, putting the first satellite into orbit. Although the feat surprised the world, it was not at all out of the blue. The Soviet satellite program was well known, and in fact, on Oct. 2, two day before the launching, the *New York Times* had a front-page article on the Russian satellite program entitled "Light May Flash in Soviets' Moon."

The military-industrial complex used Sputnik to create a hysteria that would later morph into the slogan of a "missile gap" between the United States and Russia. It was used once again to push for massive military spending.

The United States already had a satellite launch program, but it was fully separate operation from the top-secret ballistic missile programs, since its activities were not secret and were shared with the public and other nations. Advances that were made in the military program that would have been useful for the satellite program, were never shared. Eisenhower was quick to take action to increase the satellite program which soon expanded into the manned space program.

On the day of the news of Sputnik, Senators Stuart Symington and Henry Jackson, two of the biggest promoters of the military-industrial complex, charged that the administration was not spending enough, causing the United States to "fall behind" the Soviets.

Ironically, it was the Truman Administration which was to be blamed. While spending hundreds of millions on obsolete bombers like the pre-World-War-II-designed piston-engine, propeller-driven B-36 bomber, Truman had starved the missile program. In fact, rocket scientist Dr. Wernher Von Braun, who would later spearhead the Saturn Rocket program, said that the problem was that the United States had "no ballistic missile program worth mentioning between 1945 and 1951…our present dilemma is not due to the fact that we are not working hard enough now, but that we did not work hard enough during the first six or to ten years after the war."

The Gaither Report was authored by a group of private citizens under the title of "The Security Resources Panel of the Office of Defense Mobilization Science Advisory Committee." The committee had been originally authorized to study measures for the active and passive defense of the U.S. population in case of a nuclear attack. It morphed into a hysterical demand for massive expansion of military capability to face the Soviet threat.

The report, which was leaked to the *New York Times* two days before it was delivered to the President, in November 1957, was nothing less than an echo of the dangerous ideas of NSC-68.

This was not surprising because one of its authors was none other than Paul Nitze, the author of NSC-68. As for its chairman, Horace Rowan Gaither, he was cut from the same cloth.

A lawyer and investment banker, Gaither had variously been the administrator of the Ford Foundation, and founder of the Rand Corporation. He also was a founding member of the venture capital firm, Draper, Gaither & Anderson. Draper was William Henry Draper who also had a long career with Dillon Reed, the same investment bank where Nitze had worked. In and out of government and the military, Draper became a rabid advocate of genocidal zero population growth as co-founder of the Population Crisis Committee.

Another member of the committee was the young Andrew W. Marshall, who was at the time with the Rand Corporation, but soon moved to the Pentagon to become mentor to the advocates of the insane "Revolution in Military Affairs."

Eisenhower was enraged both at the report's findings, as well as the fact it had been leaked to the press. He refused to officially release it. While calling for more bombers, more missiles, and more nuclear bombs, it also called for investing $22 billion for bomb shelters, an enormous sum of money at the time. While it had little influence on his policy choices, it was symptomatic of the constant struggle that Eisenhower had to wage against the warhawks.

Eisenhower's final speech on the military-industrial complex serves as his own testimony that he felt he was not successful in wresting control of the nation's destiny from this danger, and that he would have to turn the baton over to President Kennedy. It is a bitter irony that among the first policy statements laid upon Kennedy's desk was the rejected Gaither report, and that one of his new National Security Staff members would be none other than Paul Nitze.

As history has shown, Kennedy learned that he too had an enemy within.

EIR Special Report

The British Empire's Global Showdown, And How To Overcome It

In the face of a potential thermonuclear World War III, a confrontation being engineered from London by a desperate British-centered financial oligarchy operating through the vast—yet often underestimated—powers of the British monarchy, EIR has produced a 104-page Special Report, documenting both the drive for war, and the war-avoidance efforts of patriotic military/intelligence circles in the U.S., and the Russian and Chinese leaderships. The British hand behind the warmongers, and the concrete economic and strategic programs which can defuse the threat, are elaborated in depth. These include the Russian proposal for collaboration on the Strategic Defense of Earth (SDE), based on Lyndon LaRouche's original Strategic Defense Initiative (SDI).

The Global Showdown report is available in hard copy for $250, and in pdf form for $150, from the EIR store.

Call **1-800-278-3135** for more information.

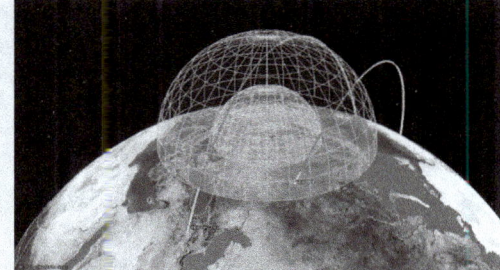

EIR
Special Report

The British Empire's Global Showdown, and How To Overcome It

June 2015

Why We Didn't Go to Nuclear War in 1962

by Jeffrey Steinberg

Aug. 3—In late October 1962, the world stood on the brink of thermonuclear war. In reaction to the Bay of Pigs invasion, Soviet Premier Nikita Khrushchov dispatched Soviet nuclear weapons to Cuba. For 13 days in October 1962, the danger of a thermonuclear war between the two superpowers was greater than at any moment until today.

Hardline advisors to both President John Kennedy and Khrushchov pressed for a confrontation, which ran the risk of triggering a thermonuclear war which would probably have ended human civilization for centuries,—even if it would have been tame compared to what we face today.

Fortunately, John F. Kennedy had a deep sense of the awesome responsibilities he carried as the ultimate decision-maker on whether humanity would live or die in an exchange of thermonuclear weapons.

From the day after John Kennedy's election as President, he entered into a secret correspondence with Khrushchov. Between November 1960 and November 20, 1963, Kennedy and Khrushchov exchanged over 100 private communiqués. While some were formal diplomatic exchanges, early in their correspondence, they agreed that some of their letters back and forth should be private, personal, and non-binding. They sought nothing more than a free channel through which to put ideas on the table, without any public scrutiny or Cabinet meddling, in order to take a better measure of one another and, above all else, to avoid war.

On Oct. 16, 1961, President Kennedy wrote to Premier Khrushchov from his vacation home at Hyannis Port, Massachusetts. The letter perfectly summarized the situation that both leaders faced.

'A Special Responsibility'

President Kennedy wrote:

I am gratified by your letter and your decision to suggest this additional means of communication. Certainly you are correct in emphasizing that this correspondence must be kept wholly private, not to be hinted at in public statements, much less disclosed to the press. For my part the contents and even the existence of our letters will be known only to the Secretary of State and a few others of my closest associates in the government. I think it is very important that these letters provide us with an opportunity for a personal, informal but meaningful exchange of views. There are sufficient channels now existing between our two governments for the more formal and official communications and

U.S. State Department

Premier Nikita Khrushchov (left) and President John F. Kennedy getting acquainted in Vienna, Austria on June 3, 1961.

public statements of position. These letters should supplement those channels, and give us each a chance to address the other in frank, realistic and fundamental terms. Neither of us is going to convert the other to a new social, economic or political point of view. Neither of us will be induced by a letter to desert or subvert his own cause. So these letters can be free from the polemics of the cold war debate. That debate will, of course, proceed, but you and I can write messages which will be directed only to each other.

The importance of this additional attempt to explore each other's view is well-stated in your letter; and I believe it is identical to the motivation for our meeting in Vienna. Whether we wish it or not, and for better or worse, we are the leaders of the world's two greatest rival powers, each with the ability to inflict great destruction on the other and to do great damage to the rest of the world in the process. We therefore have a special responsibility—greater than that held by any of our predecessors in the pre-nuclear age—to exercise our power with the fullest possible understanding of the other's vital interests and commitments. As you say in your letter, the solutions to the world's most dangerous problems are not easily found—but you and I are unable to shift to anyone else the burden of finding them.

Premier Khrushchov had wasted no time in setting about taking a measure of the newly elected American President. On Nov. 9, 1960, Khrushchov sent a revealing note of contratulations to JFK, which began:

ESTEEMED MR. KENNEDY, Allow me to congratulate you on the occasion of your election to the high post of the President of the United States.

We hope that while you are at this post the relations between our countries would again follow the line along which they were developing in Franklin Roosevelt's time, which would meet the basic interests not only of the peoples of the U.S.S.R. and the United States but all mankind which is longing for deliverance from the threat of a new war.

I think you will agree that the eyes of many people are fixed on the United States and the Soviet Union because the destinies of world

White House/Cecil Stoughton
President Kennedy and his brother, U.S. Attorney General Robert Kennedy, confer at the White House, on October 3, 1962.

peace depend largely on the state of Soviet-American relations.

In the Moment of Crisis

By the time the Cuban Missile Crisis began in the second half of October 1962, Kennedy and Khrushchov had exchanged 60 communiqués through the personal channel they had established early in Kennedy's term. The last of the pre-Cuban Missile Crisis communications was an Oct. 8, 1962 letter from JFK, responding to a Khrushchov proposal relating to ongoing negotiations on a nuclear test ban treaty, a first-ever binding agreement between the two thermonuclear superpowers, to pull back from the expansion of overkill arsenals of nuclear weapons.

During the crisis itself, JFK established a personal direct channel through his brother Robert. On October 23, hidden in the back of an associate's car so as to avoid detection, RFK made a secret visit to Soviet Ambassador Anatoly Dobrynin. The height of the crisis came on the evening of October 27. As they recalled their private thoughts afterwards, that was an evening when some inner-circle Administration officials were asking themselves whether or not they would live to see another Saturday night.

RFK asked Dobrynin to meet him in his office at the Justice Department. According to Dobrynin's report to Moscow, Robert Kennedy emphasized that time was of the essence: this chance must not be missed. He communicated a secret offer, known only to nine U.S. officials, to withdraw U.S. missiles from Turkey in exchange for the Russian missiles in Cuba. In principle, the crisis was solved.

Nixon: A Mad President is Constrained from Launching War While Being Removed

by Jeffrey Steinberg

Aug. 4—In 1967, the 25th Amendment was ratified. For the first time, it provided for the removal of a President from office, in the event he or she is judged physically or mentally unfit to continue to serve. Under the provisions, the Vice President, plus a majority of the Cabinet, was empowered to invoke the 25th Amendment and remove the President from office. If the President contested the decision, provisions further allowed for a Congressional vote to make the ultimate determination.

When Richard Nixon was going through the final phases of the Watergate investigation, there was concern among leading White House officials, including White House Chief of Staff Gen. Alexander Haig, National Security Advisor Henry Kissinger, and others, that the President was dangerously unstable. They rightly feared that Nixon might order dangerous military actions or worse, so that Defense Secretary Schlesinger personally ordered the Chairman of the Joint Chiefs of Staff (JCS), "If the President calls you, don't do what he says," according to author William Quandt.

This was not a rogue action. In effect, according to sources close to those events, the instructions to the JCS were part of the process, spelled out in the 25th Amendment for potentially removing Nixon from office. Although Nixon ultimately decided to resign, rather than face certain impeachment in a Senate trial— or removal by the provisions of the 25th Amendment,— the first case in which the 25th Amendment was put in play was the Watergating of Richard Nixon.

On at least one other occasion, the 25th Amendment was activated. That involved President Ronald Reagan. According to his own account, former Senator Howard Baker, who took over as Reagan's White House Chief of Staff in the midst of the Iran-Contra scandal of Reagan's second term, was told, upon taking the job, that

The Richard M. Nixon Library & Museum

President Nixon meets with Chief of Staff Alexander Haig (right) and National Security Adviser/Secretary of State Henry Kissinger (left) in the White House on November 13, 1972.

his first assignment was to determine whether Reagan was fit mentally to continue to serve out the remainder of his term. Baker recounted his trepidations about the first Cabinet meeting he attended as Chief of Staff. He was to make an initial judgment whether or not President Reagan should be removed under the 25th Amendment. To his great relief, Reagan walked into the Cabinet meeting room and immediately cracked a series of funny jokes. Baker concluded that the President had all his marbles.

In the Nixon case, the merit of the 25th Amendment, whichy had just been recently ratified, was clear. President Nixon was caught in the Watergate coverup trap, and he had no way out—except to launch either a foreign war or a domestic coup. His desperation, at times, bordered on madness, and it was precisely such a context, following the assassination of President John F. Kennedy, that prompted several leading Members of Congress, led by Sen. Birch Bayh, to draft the 25th Amendment.

Schubert's Ninth Symphony Brings Surprise to Manhattan

by Renée Sigerson

July 31—There are ringing out in upper midtown Manhattan these days, the voices of politically active New Yorkers, first singing, and then listening to critical musical passages of Franz Schubert's posthumous and great work, his Ninth Symphony; whereby, following upon this exercise, there emerge citizens who proceed with more vigor and self-confidence to engage their minds in dialogue with Lyndon LaRouche, on the urgent matter of the necessary actions to counter the crisis we are moving to solve, than the same people showed before they participated in this musical exercise.

Here we see that this work of Schubert, once again, has been brought forward as an instrument to shape a change in the direction of history. A moment of reflection on the circumstances associated with this composition's unique role in history may prove helpful in sustaining this process in Manhattan and other locations as well.

Some aspects of the story are well known, others not.

In 1837, the German pianist, journalist, and composer Robert Schumann—a man known for deep political convictions—undertook a trip to Vienna, Austria. According to his own account, while standing in long, awed silence between the two gravestones of Ludwig von Beethoven and Franz Schubert, Schumann was overcome by a strong desire to visit someone who knew these two heroes of his life, whom he deeply regretted never to have known in person. He resolved then to walk to the home of Schubert's brother Ferdinand, with whom he had exchanged correspondence in his magazine, hoping to share with him profound thoughts concerning the loss of these very special men.

When Ferdinand allowed him to open the chest of his brother's unpublished music manuscripts, Schumann was overcome with an all-encompassing but eerie sense of joy. (He used the word *Freudeschauernd*.) "Who knows," he later wrote, "how long the

Symphony ... would have remained covered with dust in the dark, had I not quickly agreed with Ferdinand to send it to Leipzig to the directors of the Gewandhaus," a leading German musical institution, where it was handed over to the composer and conductor Felix Mendelssohn. Schumann added, that while the Viennese loved Schubert's songs, of which he had written over 600, Schubert's symphonic works had barely ever been performed. Schumann warned: "Whoever does not know his Symphony knows little of Schubert himself."

But most important for current purposes in retelling this somewhat well-known story, is Schumann's observation that, following Beethoven's death in 1828, it had come to be assumed that *never again, would anyone else ever be able to write another symphony with the kind of "decisive influence upon the masses, as upon the progress of the species" which Beethoven's nine symphonies had uniquely accomplished.* (emphasis added-rs) It was as if human progress had come to a grinding halt. As Schumann stated, composers in general had become convinced that "after Beethoven, stay away from symphonic plans;" and that those who attempted to write symphonies came across, at best, like academic students who were attempting to imitate previous composers; or, even worse, like madmen such as the degenerate Hector Berlioz.

Schubert's Ninth Symphony, the score of which was sitting for nearly a decade in a pile of dust, was the first example of a truly great symphonic work which was "independent" of any maudlin efforts to simply mimic Beethoven. "We see here how correctly Schubert's genius manifests itself," Schumann wrote, as the composition "leads us to a region, where we previously have nothing to remember of having been there before." Despite its extended breadth, the composition has "life in every thread" and meaning everywhere.

The genius Franz Schubert (1797-1828), as depicted by Wilhelm August Rieder in 1825.

Into the Twentieth Century

Schumann knew he could unleash this powerful demonstration of human creativity under the trustworthy baton of Felix Mendelssohn, himself an original but rigorous composer. Unfortunately, by the time of the advent of the recording industry in the Twentieth Century, the moral sense and knowledge of what Schubert had accomplished with this composition was by and large lost. With only one exception, recordings of this perfected and powerful work tend to be silly, to the point of being boring and trivial, because modern musicians are incapable of detecting the principle underlying the organization of Schubert's ideas.

Lyndon LaRouche has emphasized that throughout the Twentieth Century, the only conductor who recognized the intense flame of genius at work in this composition was Wilhelm Furtwängler, whose determination to always perform music "between" as opposed to "on" the notes, is the pre-requisite for any intelligible attempt at this composition.

In the 1980s and 1990s, Lyndon LaRouche held extended, in-depth discussions on the questions of musical composition and performance, and the importance of music for civilization, with a dear friend, violinist Dr. Norbert Brainin. The founder of the only string quartet (The Amadeus Quartet) that successfully performed the full repertoire of compositions of Ludwig von Beethoven, Brainin publicly stated that LaRouche was the only person he had ever met who truly grasped the underlying principle of successful musical composition, a principle which Brainin named (in German) *Motivführung*, best translated as "motivic thorough-composition."

It was in the context of reporting on his discussions with Brainin, that LaRouche first emphasized to colleagues his long-standing recognition of the importance of Furtwängler's performance of Schubert's Ninth Symphony. Brainin demonstrated—and this in no way contradicts Schumann's stress on the importance of Schubert's *independent* method of composition relative to Beethoven's works—that the common *root* of compositional approach shared by Beethoven and Schubert, is to be found in Beethoven's Seventh Symphony, the work Brainin identified as the beginning point of Beethoven's "late" period of scientifically driven intervention into the domain of human creativity.

Brainin is unique among musicians in pointing to the Seventh Symphony—usually mischaracterized by foolish gossips as a "romantic" composition—as the beginning of a period in Beethoven's life, when he challenged musician and layman alike to open their hearts and minds to the power of music as the language of human creative activity, as opposed to any kind of stimulant of physical sensation. These compositions of Beethoven have a distinct personality.

Among musicians of that period, Schubert was the most astute in grasping what Beethoven was doing. But unlike contemporaries, he did not "mimic" Beethoven's unique personality; he internalized the method by which Beethoven had crafted this personality, and drove himself with great passion to discover greater implications of Beethoven's work within his own mind. As Schumann noted: he was successful in inspiring an effect among masses of people, when his Ninth Symphony was presented correctly; those whose admiration of Beethoven moved in the direction of doctrinaire copying of external characteristics of

Beethoven's "style," had no such effect.

There are many implications to Brainin's discussions with LaRouche on Beethoven's works, and the actual way they inspired other composers, not to be doctrinaire copyists of Beethoven's efforts, but to drive their own potential for discovery.

For now, suffice it to say that the concept of "motivic thorough-composition" recognizes that a pair or collection of musical intervals functions like a seed-crystal. Seeds spring forth into living organisms. Music is the language of the human mind, and the harmonic intervals between tones, in pairs and sequences, have the potential to generate a living process, which is what an idea really should be. In the mind of a great composer, musical intervals are "embryonic," with broad implications for unfolding a unified process of development. It requires tremendous concentration and love of humanity to drive that process forward; and if successfully presented, the effect is to transplant that underlying determination to bring this result to life, into a higher sense of purpose among human beings. In that sense, as Furtwängler noted repeatedly, the real subject of music is love.

That is why the enemies of mankind always try to crush real music and impose low forms of "entertainment" upon potentially resistant populations. That is why this new phase in the life of Schubert's Ninth Symphony, as a companion to the Manhattan Project launched by LaRouche to save the United States, has so many promising implications.

LaRouche Policy Committee member Diane Sare's approach, to have participants at Manhattan's Saturday Dialogue with Lyndon LaRouche sing *before* the meeting, has had a deep-going effect. The centerpiece of this work is to open the door for every political supporter to personally experience why LaRouche has placed so much emphasis upon Schubert's Ninth as an historically important composition, but also to demonstrate that it is only in Furtwängler's performances of this work that you can legitimately say, "this composition still lives!"

Creativity occurs within the sovereign recesses of the individual human mind; as valuable as known ideas may be, creativity does not exist in dogmatic repetition of formulas, a distinction to which Schumann was committed without compromise. Yet,—and it seems to be a paradox,—true creativity is intensely "social," or

"Whoever does not know his Symphony knows little of Schubert himself," stated composer Robert Schumann, who discovered the symphony in 1837. Here, Schumann with his wife and fellow artist Clara Wieck Schumann.

only validated as part of a social process. The paradox is only apparent, not real. Music is the historically grounded medium through which the bridge is formed between the creative processes of discovery unfolded in an individual mind, and the mental processes of large numbers of people, in the context of a real "musical event." Once a human being has experienced this process in its living form, its lingering effect takes hold of every aspect of that person's mental life. Such uplifting experiences can easily be overwhelmed in a degenerate culture, however, which is why the process of weekly efforts in this direction is so important to rebuilding the kind of national mission of the United States which it has embodied under its greatest Presidents.

What Is Mankind's Mission?

August 1, 2015

Dennis Speed:: My name is Dennis Speed, and I'd like to welcome everybody here for today's dialogue with Lyndon LaRouche. We're going to start right in. Mr. LaRouche has an opening statement, and we'll start with questions immediately thereafter. So, Lyn?

Lyndon LaRouche: Yes. This operation we're doing here in Manhattan has a very significant meaning to it. First of all, Manhattan actually is the real capital of the United States. Now, some people may quarrel about that, but I can assure you that that's the fact, and we're talking about the initiation of the George Washington administration; but then you had another man [Alexander Hamilton] who was also making that all possible. So that is extremely important, and it's important to recognize what that principle is.

Because that principle is the principle on which the United States was put into motion, actually in motion, on behalf of George Washington in particular. And that is the standard which we sometimes lose track of, especially in the course of history, because there have been a number of Presidents after Washington—about four of them—who were really not deserving of the position of that; then we had one or two good Presidents, and then we had a bunch of bums, more or less; and then we got into Abraham Lincoln, and then we got a great general [Ulysses Grant], who finished his military service as such, and he became a President of the United States with two terms of office.

So, there is an unresolved problem inside the existence of our United States: that we've had some great Presidents, who have some great movements, Presidential movements, terms of office in general. We've had a lot of bums. And we are, in the Twentieth Century, fortunate in one or two Presidents, or actually three, and we got a lot of bums; especially after Franklin Roosevelt left office, things began to get very bad.

And now, the condition of the United States is *horrible*. There's a general deterioration in the mental life of our citizenry, since a decline which began at the beginning of the Twentieth Century. We have been going downhill, worse and worse, in our mental life, and the effects of our mental life in terms of voices, exchanges, and so forth. And so, we would hope that by going back to a reference to a great President, and to a great man

> **We're now on the edge of the greatest threat to human existence throughout the planet, right now. With Obama still in the Presidency, we're in the danger of being dragged into a thermonuclear war, a global thermonuclear war, from which very few people, if any, would actually survive.**

U.S. Army/Sgt. Alexander Skripnichuk

FLASHPOINT: U.S. troops maneuver with Ukrainian troops in the Rapid Trident exercise on July 27, 2015—one of an escalating set of U.S. and NATO maneuvers being carried out on the Russian border.

who backed him up, that we can recover the meaning of the Presidency of the United States, as under its first President.

That, to me, is crucial, because unless we can achieve that, and get rid of some of the mistakes that came in during the Twentieth Century, and now in this present century ongoing, we've been going downhill, morally, intellectually, otherwise, in general. And my hope is that by going back to Alexander Hamilton's standard of performance, his great genius,—that by going back to reach that level, which was the level reached by the best people in Manhattan, that the spirit of Manhattan, carried from that time, can be reaffirmed.

And that's what my mission is, here in particular. We're now on the edge of the greatest threat to human existence throughout the planet, right now. We're now presently, with Obama still in the Presidency, in danger of being dragged into a thermonuclear war, a global thermonuclear war, from which very few people, if any, would actually survive, even the very brief introduction of that war. So, my immediate concern is to prevent that thermonuclear war, which would virtually exterminate the human species. And, my concern is to get Obama out of office, because the existence of Obama—if continued during this last month—would be the death of most of humanity, and the death of the meaning of all the history that's come before.

So, I think that we, who represent a selection of some people (and more), who are devoted to that mission, may be the forces which will lead the way, to escape from the monstrous conditions that threaten us, under the continuation of the Obama Administration.

Q: Good afternoon, this is A— from New York. Your recent remarks regarding this very threat of thermonuclear war—you mentioned that we had a very narrow period of options coming up, as the summer progresses; and then we have—I wonder if you could help clarify the provocations and the set-up that's taking place within Syria; Turkey's involvement in that, and how the United States has been coming out now, and is continuing its provocations and pivot into Russia.

The Russians have been very clear that they're monitoring this; they're very well aware of it and ready to respond. Now, in our government, we are getting the response and echoes, and a fight around Glass-Steagall—we're aware of that—but we're not hearing anything, from anybody, in the form of leadership about this threat. We know, through you, that the Joint Chiefs of Staff are doing all they can to avoid this, but of course, Obama has this window now with Congress out.

So, I'm wondering if you could help us further understand. What particularly I'm wondering about is what is going on in Syria with the Turks, the threat of a no-fly zone (which is an act of war), and just more in terms of what's required in terms of leadership within our house to remove Obama?

Obama Threatens Russia, and Us All

LaRouche: Well, the basic thing that has to happen,—the keystone comes from Russia. Russia's gone through a lot of history; I've enjoyed, shall we say, some of the taste of Russia's decline, and its attempt to bounce back up. I was active in those efforts, on behalf of Russia, after the post-Soviet period.

And, I was able to make contributions. I was associated in that effort with Bill Clinton, when he was President, during the first term and what was left of the second term after the British Monarchy got through with him, and others.

So, these conditions are ones I understand very well. And I understand precisely what the problem is: that if Obama were to have his druthers—. And now, you have to realize that Obama is merely a patsy, he's a patsy for the British Empire; that's what he belongs to, why he got his job as President. And as long as he remains in control, willful control over the policies of the United States, we are now sitting proximately to the extermination, or virtual extermination, of most of the human species.

Because, in one case, the war issue is defined by only one issue: Russia, including China as a part of the picture. But Russia and the United States are the essential elements which threatens the extermination of the human species. And, it is likely, that it would be possible, or likely possible, that once Obama—if he's successful—launches a war against Russia—Russia will not launch a war.

But if the United States, under Obama, launches a war, then in response to the launching of a war by the Obama Administration, then we have a *global* thermonuclear war; in which it's doubtful that humanity, as we've known it heretofore, would survive even the initial launching of such a thermonuclear war.

Back in history, there was a time when a great President dealt with Russia, in a recent time out of the Cuba business; and this President—this Presiden*cy*—protected the United States, and the world, from a thermo-

If Obama is able to maintain control over the policies of the United States, during the period of this month, then the doom of most of our nation, and most of the planet will go down with it. That is what must be prevented, and that is what I'm dedicated to prompt the people who should know better, to know better, and to do the things to get Obama thrown out of office, and to realize a great peace.

FLASHPOINT: Ukrainian fascist groups which have been supported by Obama and NATO, rally against President Poroshenko on July 22, 2015, demanding a more aggressive policy against Russia.

nuclear holocaust. The government of Russia destroyed its own nuclear arsenal, in order to secure peace and avoidance of war, and a great President of ours, who was to be assassinated pretty soon, did the job to negotiate that peace.

Now, we're in a situation where Obama, who's merely a stooge for the British Empire in fact, but he's the agent right now; and if Obama is able to maintain control over the policies of the United States, during the period of this month, then the doom of most of our nation, and most of the planet will go down with it. That is what must be prevented, and that is what I'm dedicated to: prompting the people who should know better, to know better, and to do the things to get Obama thrown out of office, and to realize a great peace. As great Presidents who had been general officers during World War II *did* take the actions to prevent a thermonuclear war; as Kennedy did take the action to prevent a thermonuclear war of that nature.

But now, who's going to defend us against what Obama represents? And, the question is, in my mind, are there still members of the Congress, and other institutions of the United States as such, which will kindly throw Obama out of office, so that we can avoid a general thermonuclear destruction of, among other nations, our own United States?

No Alternative to Removing Obama

Q: Hi, Mr. LaRouche. This is H— from the Bronx. Today we have the news about the apparent default on $58 million payment of a Puerto Rican corporation, or "state corporation"; and this also involves hedge funds who are demanding austerity, cuts in education, and so on. And, I know that you are familiar with the Puerto Ricans in New York. I once read your paper on the Puerto Rican Socialist Party, and the funny relationship between the Puerto Ricans in the United States, who now outnumber the Puerto Ricans on the island.

Also I was reviewing that the collapse of Puerto Rico dates particularly to the 1996 period, when they lost certain tax benefits, and they lost their petrochemical industries, and their pharmaceutical industries; and this is also at the same time that we lost our Glass-Steagall, when we had free trade agreements, our NAFTA and so on. So, I was wondering, what is your opinion about these questions of trade and development for Puerto Rico, and also as a potential flank against our situation right now?

LaRouche: The Puerto Rican situation is one of a great injustice. That's a fact! Now, the fact that there is a great injustice in that case, what do we do about it? What *can* we do about it? Well, there's nothing we can do about it, unless we get Obama out of the Presidency! Nothing you can do, for Puerto Rico, as long as Obama remains in the Presidency. And there are a lot of other parts of the planet which are threatened similarly to Puerto Rico.

Now, the point is, you can say, you want to fight for that cause. Well, can you win that fight? To win that

FLASHPOINT: *U.S. guided-missile destroyers in the Pacific Ocean have been deployed by Obama in maneuvers threatening China, in the South China Sea and environs.*

U.S. Navy

fight for Puerto Rico, you must remove Obama from the Presidency; otherwise you're not going to succeed.

That's mostly true for other parts of the world, especially the trans-Atlantic community. France is going into a disaster. Hopefully, the British Empire, the British Monarchy, will be shut down, early, because it was the British Monarchy which had actually organized Obama and created the Obama hate business.

So these are the kinds of problems, and we cannot take a particular issue under these conditions and say that there's one place which is the most important place, to give relief to around the planet, or around the Americas. There is no such choice.

If you get rid of Obama and what he represents, *then* the gate to freeing Puerto Rico is possible. If you depend on somebody else, some other way, to try to rescue Puerto Rico, you're wasting your time. Unless you can remove both the British Empire, and in particular, Obama—who is nothing but an agent of the British Empire—you cannot save Puerto Rico in any way.

That's the challenge: Are you willing to concentrate on taking action of a type which will actually solve the *general* problem? Don't try to pick one local issue, however important it may be. Don't presume that you can devote yourself to concentrate only on Puerto Rico, for example, or other situations similarly. *That will not work.* You must, first of all, remove Obama from the Presidency. Otherwise, you can't succeed.

Q: Good afternoon, Mr. LaRouche. I wish to introduce at this moment a musical question for you, because I'm concerned to run down the scholarly background to J.S. Bach's use of the tuning pitch of 432.

We know that he did not use this in Leipzig; he couldn't. His organ was tuned a half a step higher than 440, and J.S. Bach himself had his singers and instrumentalists playing at a half tone below; and the organ part, if the cantata were, let's say, in D minor, would be copied out in C minor, a whole tone lower, so that it would be consonant with the singers.

But you see he couldn't go to 430, which apparently is what he wanted, I would gather from reading Kepler—I know that one of Kepler's books was in his library. So that would explain my reading, years ago, that both Quantz and Bach favored 430, but I haven't been able to run that down.

We are in contact with the greatest living Bach scholar, Prof. Christian Wolff of Harvard, and he's promised to try to look into it, to find out where this came from. I'm convinced it came from Kepler.

The point is that Bach was not able to tune at 430 simply because the organ was too high. You tune it down half a step, you get 440. You tune it down another half a step—you can't tune it down by micro-tones obviously—and you've got 415, a half-tone below, which is where Bach operated all the time he was in Leipzig.

The question is, where is the scholarly proof that Bach advocated 430 or 432? I seem to have read that, but I can't get to the source. Can you help me out, here?

Between the Notes

LaRouche: Well, I think so. I can give you an indication of which way to look at it. Look, Bach understood what he was doing. He understood the intentions.

Now the point is, where the problem arises, is when people try to take the string values of tones; that often is a mistake. Because the real issue, the underlying issue, which deals with the question of Bach, essentially, is the placement of the singing voice, as opposed to the placement of the note. In other words, this distinction between the placing of the voice, the singing voice, and the placement of the note are not exactly the same thing.

Otherwise, everything is true as what was done by our great Italian musicians, who did much of the work, most influential work, which I was exposed to, considerably, during my visits in Europe. But that does prevail.

But! Verdi—Verdi had a deep insight into the true principle of Bach. But the principle is not located on the note as such. It's located in the placement—the placement, like in Furtwängler's treatment of Schubert's Ninth Symphony. You notice very carefully in the opening section of that piece, you see very clearly how Furtwängler approached the problem, by playing *between* the notes, *not* on the notes. And if you look carefully, also, you will see that Giuseppe Verdi also had a similar approach.

I never met Verdi personally, but I was part of a memorandum on his work, and it was held by the people of Italy, the best Italian performers. So that's the situation: The placement of the note, *between* the notes, is the solution for the problem.

Otherwise, the approximations which can be achieved in that way, are relevant to that. But, if you tune into the note,—*on* the note you may miss the precise point—that's important. You'll find this in the best of great singers and performers. You'll see that. The best performers work not *on* the note, but *between* the notes. And that's where the placement lies.

Q: Thank you. Good afternoon, Mr. LaRouche. This is J— from Brooklyn. I remember in the past that you've talked about strategy and outflanking the enemy. So I'm just curious: what would you say about advancing Glass-Steagall through interventions in the state assembly districts, not to create a local initiative but to force the legislators to take a position that aligns with O'Malley or Sanders, or even someone on the Republican side like Rick Perry, who is a total character, but he has, at least, come out with something positive about Glass-Steagall very recently. So, what would you think about that type of strategy?

LaRouche: I would say you're pretty much working in the right direction, toward the right goal. There are technical things, and details, which are specific. But for your purpose, in raw terms of your stated question, I would say that's the case. You can accept that.

Speed: Yes. I will refrain from making a comment about that because I was thinking that about Glass-Steagall myself. Can you go ahead, M—, with your question?

White House/Pete Souza

FLASHPOINT: Obama's alliance with radical Islamic groups, from Libya to Syria, threatens to blow up into global conflict. Here Obama confers with another NATO sponsor of the jihadis, Turkish then-Prime Minister Recep Tayyip Erdogan, in September 2009.

Lessons of Obama's Benghazi Treachery

Q: Hi, Lyn, hi. It's M—, born in Manhattan. You put forth how important it is for the safety of the country, that we, in the next week—that would be the best—somehow or other prompt Hillary Clinton to come clean on Benghazi, to admit what was really going on. Frankly it was easy; I knew it when it happened.

The whole process of shipping the arms to al-Qaeda, and probably to ISIS through Turkey, through Benghazi. Benghazi was the seat of al-Qaeda, and my sons, veterans who were in that war, were devastated when they found that there really was no adequate protection for Ambassador Stevens. My other friend, who is Turkish, she said to me, "You were so right, 187 villagers, Turkish villagers along the border, have been murdered, M—!" And I told her this when it happened, that these were no rebels.

What would you suggest? How can we go about getting Senator Clinton,—she was the Senator when 9/11 happened, and when the parents and the wives and the husbands had to see these buildings come down on their loved ones; how can we get her to come forward and admit that it was an inside job, Benghazi?

LaRouche: Of course, it was an inside job. It was a complete inside job, but Hillary got to a point, and I think you probably have seen some of the record on this; what was reported at the time, where Obama had actually set up the assassination of officials of the United States in that area. Obama did it, and his crew of women also did it.

Now, Hillary was a different case, but also her complications are really significant on this account. She resisted at first, resisted Obama's intention. Now Obama was the one who set this thing up. And if you don't focus on Obama, and concentrate on getting him thrown out of office immediately—that is, in the immediate future, before he can start the war that he intends to launch, or the British and other kinds of sources.

Under those conditions, Hillary is a very doubtful person, morally. She is a stooge for Obama. She became a stooge for Obama because she wanted to serve under him, and that was her mistake. And she didn't realize what she was getting into when she got into it. But she's a person of ambition, of political ambition, and therefore she made mistakes in various ways, which showed a problem in her judgment, a systemic problem in her making of judgments.

So now, what e're left with is the fact that if we don't get rid of Obama, from the Presidency during this month, you're probably going to all be dead or something like dead, within the course of this month. That's what the threat is. In other words, it's not a question of raising a protest. It's a question of getting this guy *thrown* out of power. Getting him thrown out of power will do the job.

We had histories of that. After Franklin Roosevelt's death, we had a couple of Presidents, of military background, who actually did make a great contribution to preventing the United States from being involved in major wars. About three Presidents, in particular, intervened to prevent war; I think other Presidents had also made a contribution in that direction.

The problem now is that Obama is a British agent, in fact; that is, he got his post through the British Empire, the Queen herself, and he's now,—because he was able to pull this swindle by getting Hillary to sell herself, sell her soul virtually. She got out of office, she walked out of the office, yes. But she refused to tell the truth, even though she *knew* what the truth was. She *knew* it, and we have it on the record.

Bill Clinton had been beside her at the time that this discussion occurred. And she just flubbed it, and then she just went out and began to get more decayed in her judgment, her morality and judgment. And there are a lot of things you could say about her, if you want to write a book about Hillary and her experience in life; that's a whole story in itself. But I'd say the simple thing is, that Hillary has so far failed her obligation to save the United States, from the *horrible* thing that

---

Hillary has so far failed her obligation to save the United States, from the horrible thing that Obama is about to bring down on the entire United States, and more.

Obama is about to bring down on the entire United States, and more.

Musical Placement and Morality

Speed: I just wanted to say one thing, which just came to mind when you were talking to T—. There was a documentary that's done on Furtwängler. It's up on YouTube; it's available, and it has a lot of valuable footage. But it has a very specific story, which is told by a critic and a musician, Hans Keller, I think is his name.

Anyway he tells a story that Furtwängler once attended a performance of the Ninth Symphony by Toscanini. What happened was that he heard the opening phrases; he got up out of his seat; he shouted, "Bloody time-beater," and walked out. Now Keller says, what had happened was, Toscanini was taking the opening phrases, which are in the sextuplets, and he was playing the notes. And he said, that was because he wanted to be precise. He said, "Furtwängler does the opposite." And within the documentary they play the two performances; he says, because Furtwängler understood that *imprecision* "was what Beethoven wanted, that the idea here was a completely different musical idea, and that the idea was the opening before the opening." That's how he says it, that's what Keller says.

But the more important thing was—I just wanted to insert this because of what you were saying to T— before—this issue of placement, and how you talk about it. Because you've also outlined a project for people here, although you saw part of it, around the chorus, and what the purpose of it is.

Why do you think this is so central to doing exactly the things you are asking us to do politically?

LaRouche: Modern civilization, particularly since the beginning of the Twentieth Century was a disaster for the people in Europe and the United States, as well—a moral disaster, but a moral disaster with strong characteristics, as worse things to do.

Technically, the point is, what every great musician, composer, knew, was the principle of Bach, and the principle of those who followed Bach, such as Mozart, notably, Beethoven, and so forth, up through Brahms. This was very well known. There were differences in the way they approached something, but that was not a contradiction in their effort; it was a different expres-

---

What is the principle which makes a composition, of music, for example, beautiful? And what otherwise is not beautiful? That is the placement of the tone which is between the notes; not on the notes, between the notes.

---

sion, but based on following: for example, Beethoven followed Mozart. Beethoven was followed by such great people as Brahms. Brahms ended his life within the context of the Nineteenth Century.

And then suddenly Furtwängler came along, and Furtwängler provided the means to continue the mission, which had been handed down through Brahms. In other words, Furtwängler was actually a follower, in that sense, of Brahms. That is, he added something to what Brahms had accomplished, and it was beyond the achievement of Brahms himself.

So, that's the way to look at these kinds of things. What's the point here? The point is there's a principle, the principle of music among other things—the Classical principle. Why do we say, not *on* the note? Why *between* the notes? Why do we say *between* the notes? Because the significance of music, when it's decent music, when it's good music, is that the tone is placed between the notes. That is, in the movement from one note to the next note, and so forth and so on, there's a process which identifies the meaning, the actual meaning of the performance, and the way the performance is composed. And that's the principle.

So, the problem is, that most people today, do not have any actual efficient comprehension of what that means, and unfortunately we have terrible music, and we have also terrible science. They're both incompetent. Physical science, as defined by almost everybody in the Twentieth Century and today, is rotten, from the standpoint of science, because they don't know that principle that human beings. . . .

Yes, they do have tones; they do place tones, and things like that, but that's not the answer. The answer is, what is the principle which makes a composition, of music, for example, what makes it beautiful? and what otherwise is not beautiful? And that is the placement of the tone which is *between* the notes; not *on* the notes, *between* the notes. And the fact that the orchestration of performance lies between the notes rather than on the notes.

Satanic Bush vs. Alexander Hamilton

Q: Hello, Mr. LaRouche, I have a question about a different type of note, actually, specific to our currency. I was wondering if you could comment on a recent item that's been in the news, and that's been removing Alexander Hamilton from the $10 note and replacing him instead with one of our amazing women? And if you feel it would be better, perhaps, to remove Andrew Jackson from the $20 note and put somebody new there instead?

LaRouche: Obviously, we've got to get rid of Jackson. Jackson was one of the most evil men who ever occupied the Presidency. The man was a Satanic kind of character. And if you look at his history, this man was intrinsically Satanic, in everything about him; and also his successor, equally Satanic. And that's the way to look at it—this guy; you don't want to waste time on him, once you know that he's Satanic. You don't need to run around.

The problem is: In the history of the Presidency, we had the first President, who was actually promoted by Alexander Hamilton. Hamilton was the person who orchestrated the policy of our economy, our system. The papers he wrote, the four papers that he published, are the principles of the U.S. economy: Alexander Hamilton. And Washington supported that, accepted it. But Hamilton was the genius who came up with the solution.

And over the course of the history there were occasional Presidents who were of that kind of commitment. I will not go into the whole list, but there were a number of that character. And I honor those men, in particular. They were great Presidents.

And unfortunately since the Bush family began to invade the Presidency of the United States. . . . You have to understand, that the Bush family—the boys, shall we say—were really jokers, totally incompetent, stupid jerks; but they came from a father, Prescott Bush, who's quite capably Satanic, purely Satanic. And anyone who knows that history, knows that what you had, was a certain kind of punishment of Prescott Bush. That he was a Satanic creature, but Satan played a dirty trick on him, by making all the Presidents in his name, got them to be *absolutely stupid*, as well as nasty.

Russell Destroyed Science

Q: Hi, Mr. LaRouche, how are you doing. My name is M——. Good afternoon everybody. I want to ask you, are we ever going to go back and open up the NASA program? I worked on the LEM (Lunar Excursion Module) program in Bethpage, Long Island. And during those years I was the ground support engineer liaison, the liaison engineer between ground support equipment and the vehicle. Will we ever have a program like this again, as far as NASA is concerned? The Pluto program we have now is nothing like what we had in the '60s.

LaRouche: You're right in pointing out the problem, as such, in practice, but the question is a deeper question which has to be faced. What happened at the passing point from the Nineteenth Century into the Twentieth Century—in the Twentieth Century you had predominantly Satanic forces who were in charge of science and pretty much everything else, and they were all recruited by Bertrand Russell, and Bertrand Russell was truly the true servant of Satan, if there ever was one of that type! So that's where the problem lies.

The problem is that we believe, according to the doctrine of the Twentieth Century—remember, all leading scientists, so-called scientists, of the Twentieth Century were followers of a Satanic cult: Bertrand Russell. And what happened was, there was only one person, in science, who was actually competent in physical science, not Bertrand Russell. And so the problem has been, that what we had instead of having an actual *physical* science, we had mathematical pseudo-science. And what has been taught during the Twentieth Century and now during the present century, again, is a consistent degeneration in the mental powers of the typical member of society in the United States and also in Europe. There is no competence in suggesting that

creative commons/Ibrahim Qasim

FLASHPOINT: Obama's backing of the Saudi attack on Yemen this summer, threatens an expanded conflict in the region against Iran—and then potentially against Russia and China. Here, the aftermath of a Saudi airstrike on Sana'a, June 12, 2015.

mathematics is the basis for science. That's the point. And until we get that thing corrected, we're still going to have the problem.

We may have a lesser degree of the problem, but we do not have a competent standard. We have individuals who are scientists, and they tend to feel out the principles which had been known, in the end of the Nineteenth Century. We had a period of great scientists in that period, a few great scientists, in that period, and they accomplished something. But since that time, since the beginning of the Twentieth Century, science has become fraudulent, except for Einstein.

Einstein was the one man who was truly competent as a scientist. All others are merely poor approximations of that. And that is the issue which has to be really understood and taken up, because we're going into what? We're going into Galactic studies and such. The Galactic principles are now really the principles which are now the principles which are most important for us. So we have to have a systematic change, in the way we define the meaning of science. Get rid of mathematics. Mathematics has a function, but it's not a scientific one, and that's the problem.

Q: My name is F——. I'm a political activist for years and my question is, you say that we must remove Obama, and impeach him. And I work a lot to try to get the people to know what's going on. I was involved in Clinton's impeachment proceedings. That was about the 1993 World Trade Center bombings, about the Oklahoma Federal Building controlled demolitions, and about Clinton ignoring monopoly laws, and during his impeachment proceedings, he deregulated media, leaving us with six corporate conglomerate media outlets. So, the facts of Clinton's impeachment proceedings were never brought to the public.

So how do we replace Obama? You know, it will be

All animals are animals, but human beings are not animals. Why? Because the human being, unlike any so-called natural, living personality, does not depend on practical considerations. People are going to die,—that is, the human body is very susceptible to being killed in one way or the other; but! the question is, what does mankind, while living, produce and generate, for the future benefit of mankind as a species?

---

the same thing. And how do we regulate the media, banks, and military? Those are the real problems. The real problems and the banks, the military, and the media, and the military-industrial complex and the prison-industrial complex. So, I was told to say, if we remove Obama, who's next?

Man Is Not an Animal

LaRouche: That's a pessimistic view of matters. I'm not a pessimist. I can find myself disgusted by what's going on around me, and I have been steadily, mostly disgusted by most of the things I've experienced, in my lifetime. So I've got a good record there of being disgusted about bad things. And I've always rejected, for example, mathematics. I haven't rejected it absolutely; it's a toy you can play with, but it's not science, and *that's* the issue. So, mathematics is fake science! It's the attempt to imitate, from a distance, what is really science, what we mean by physical science.

This is the same thing that just came up in the previous discussion: That mankind is unique. Mankind is not animal. And that's a very important point: Mechanical devices can be taught to perform certain kinds of procedures. These procedures which are called mathematical procedures, sometimes called science; they're *not* science. They're anti-science.

Because the question here is, what's the nature of mankind as opposed to being an animal? Well, mankind is not an animal! Animals are animals! All animals are animals, but human beings are not animals. Why? Be-

cause the human being, unlike any so-called natural, living personality, does not depend on practical considerations. The purpose of mankind is that mankind— while people are going to die, that is, the human body is very susceptible to being killed in one way or the other; *but!* the question is, what does mankind, while living, produce and generate, for the future benefit of mankind as a species?

Now, the obvious thing is that mankind is unique in that respect. We die; all human beings die. But the human principle does not die. It merely passes on to the next step, preferably the next step up. Scientific progress, *not* mathematics, real science, physical science; the discovery of new physical principles which give mankind the power, new powers, previously unknown powers to all mankind, which enable mankind to achieve things which no other species can accomplish.

And this is well known in terms of the history of religion, for example. Kepler was on one of the followers of this thing, and he was the first person to discover the Solar System. He didn't do much beyond that, because he died in the process, after having made that achievement. But the issue here, is that mankind is a being, intended by implication, to be a creative force, a creative force which can create, in itself, powers in and over mankind, in and over the Solar System, in and over the Galaxy. And mankind has those powers of discovery, of scientific discovery, *which no animal species has ever been able to duplicate.*

And the whole business of mankind, which is the actual basis of Christianity, for example, as Nicolaus of Cusa, for example, illustrates this, that there's an intention in the existence of the human species, such that even the death of a member of the human species, is not finality. What continues is the contribution of the once-living person to bring into knowledge and into practice things which mankind would never have known otherwise. New things, new discoveries.

Now today, for example, we're talking about the water problem. What about the water problem on United States, for example, or Earth in general? Well, the solution is there. The greatest supply of water for people on Earth, is provided under the control of the Galaxy, a superior body. Now it's only recently that we've begun to understand what the Galaxy is and what it does. But that's a discovery *by mankind*. That's a typical example of the progress of humanity: That we live and we die. But, if we do our work properly, we will be part of those people who make the discoveries, which enable mankind to reach new levels of achievement, just like Kepler discovered the Solar System; just like today, the Galactic System is understood to be the superior system, under which mankind's Earth operates.

So this distinction of mankind from the animal, is absolute. And therefore, what is the achievement of mankind? It's to make discoveries and to make practice of discoveries which enable the human species to accomplish something useful for the future of mankind's existence, which had never been known, or had never been *knowable* before. And that is what the real, underlying principle is; when you get through all these questions, *get* to that point!

Don't try to interpret what somebody says is their experience—forget it! People talk about their experiences, they talk about the judgments they reached by their experiences, it's bunk! Very few people, living so far as today, actually have the ability *to foresee* the meaning of human life. But nonetheless, mankind's progress to higher levels of achievement, is a symptom of the fact that mankind is a species *like no other.* And that is the principle of the Creator and the relationship of the Creator to Creation. [applause]

Discoveries That Change the Future

Q: Hi Lyn. I've had the chance to organize in Manhattan the past few weeks a couple of times, and it's a lot of fun, but it's also very difficult to engage people. And one of the difficulties is as if,—you know how Edgar Allan Poe describes in the *Purloined Letter*, where the solution to the problem is right in people's faces, especially people who are living in Manhattan and working here, because of Wall Street, 9/11, the Saudi faction, and all that; it's all around them. But they don't see it.

And I think one of the ways to overcome this problem is to show people that the reason they don't see it, is because they think mathematically, like the *Purloined Letter*. Whereas, the way to organize people is to be a poet yourself, and to show them that you have to approach your thinking, not from a mathematical deductive nature, but from a higher standpoint. And I just wanted you to comment on that, because that's what

was brought up this week by some members on our debriefings and our organizing here.

LaRouche: I'm certainly and fully in support of that argument that you make, because it's valid, absolutely valid! And I'm very glad that you exist, because it reassures me that we have some people who are really, shall we say, on the ball.

Q: Hi, Mr. LaRouche, this is E— from the Bronx. I would like to ask you, if we were able to land the rocket, manned or unmanned, on all the other planets on our

---

The issue here, is that mankind is a being, intended by implication, to be a creative force, a creative force which can create, in itself, powers in and over mankind, in and over the Solar System, in and over the Galaxy. And mankind has those powers of discovery, of scientific discovery, which no animal species has ever been able to duplicate.

Solar System, how would that improve life, or make a better life on Earth, on our planet? Is there any relevance to doing that, or would it not make a difference? … Would we be able to benefit from that? Would we learn something from that? Would we be able to make a better life for the people on Earth? Or would that not make a difference in what is going on, on our planet today?

LaRouche: [Let me redirect the] subject a little bit. Don't try to make a deduction, in the future. In other words, don't assume that you can make a deduction which will lead to a discovery of a higher principle. That's where the mistake often comes up. The problem is, that you have to see a problem, you have to see a fallacy in the nature of human behavior, currently.

In other words, mankind is perplexed, and doesn't know what the future is going to be. He knows the future has to be *in* the future, not as a product of what has happened up to now; in other words, it depends upon successful progress beyond what had been known already. A change in quality, a higher principle which corrects the error, of the assumption that we know what the answers are.

And that's called science, real science, as opposed to this fake science which is called mathematical physics; mathematical physics is a complete fraud, inherently, by very definition. Because it does not answer the question of creativity. And mankind's behavior, what distinguishes mankind from the animals, is that mankind *is* capable of making discoveries which change the

U.S. Air Force/Tech Sgt. Joseph Swafford

FLASHPOINT: Obama has kept over 10,000 U.S. troops in Afghanistan, after the so-called withdrawal of the NATO force this spring. Here U.S. soldiers enter a U.S. Army CH-47 Chinook helicopter at an Afghan combat outpost.

future, that is, the future of mankind, the future of the Solar System, the future of the Galaxy. *That's* what's important.

That means that the question is, the discovery of a new principle, which had not been known before, but it's now known and it's proven. And the idea is that every generation of mankind, in the normal course of events, must be superior, in that generation's capabilities, beyond anything that mankind had known up to now. And the idea is that pursuit of the successful pursuit, of the unknown, the unknown triumph, which is the meaning of the future.

For example, someone has made a partial scientific discovery, or some other related kind of discovery, or great poetry. New ingenuity in the concept of poetry, for example, can be very useful in this respect, but the point is, you have to have in yourself, the devotion, the efficient devotion, to make discoveries of universal principles within the universe, but which mankind had not known before.

Science Is the Measure

Q: Good afternoon. My name is R—. I'm from Brooklyn. I'd like to know, is there anything new on the British Empire and its demise? See I have a slightly different attitude from some people. Some people say, "God save the Queen." I say, "God save the Queen,

because I won't!" [laughter]

LaRouche: OK! Well, the Queen, I think, is probably on the skids right now. It's not only because she and her husband are about my age, which is an embarrassment to me, to find that at my age they still got some rumpus characters like these, the British Royal Family. But the solution is simply, in the characteristic of the British system in particular, like some Satanic kinds of religious beliefs, or similarly that way; but it's the idea that mankind treats mankind as merely something disposable, like those who say we've got too many people; we've got to reduce the population of mankind. Well, these ideas are essentially, intrinsically Satanic, and should be rejected at all times, in all places. And that's what the issue is.

The point is, mankind has a unique capability, which no other known species of life, has ever been able to manifestly achieve. Mankind is intrinsically capable of making discoveries, discoveries of principles, not just discoveries of fact; discoveries of principle, of universal physical principles, and mankind is able to do that with the help of education, with the help of hard work and things of that sort; or lucky strokes, even. And that's what's important.

When people die—you know people you know die—a great sadness comes over you in that moment of sharing the experience of the death of a person who you have cherished, or even wished they had not died, to say it simply. And the issue is, what reconciles mankind with the death of another human being? And that is a contribution to the future of mankind's development and powers to solve problems, which mankind has not understood yet, before.

That's what the principle is. What do we live for? We're all going to die. All human beings are going to die. So what's the meaning of their life? The meaning of their life is something good and new, at least for them and for humanity, which opens the gate for mankind's achievement; just like the progress of Kepler—Kepler discovered the Solar System. He was the one who discovered it, absolutely unique; no duplication known.

And thus, science in that sense is the measure of a meaning of human life. That is, the meaning of the future of the person who had died, the person whose death celebrates what they had achieved for mankind. Great art, great music, great things that impassion mankind, by which means mankind is able to muster himself, to reach out and achieve necessary discoveries and practices which will improve the future of mankind as such.

Mankind Is Going to Grow Up

Q: Good afternoon, Mr. La-Rouche, my name's A—, and I'm from New York City. I have a question I'd like to ask you: If you were the person in charge, say, starting Monday, and we wanted to know what can be done about immigration in our country today—what's going on with immigration—how would you handle it? What are the steps you would take, in sequences, and how do you think they would affect our politics, and our economy in our country?

LaRouche: Certain conclusions can be drawn right at this time. First of all, for a long period of time, we have prided ourselves on observing the achievement of great nations, and we assume that the great nations are somehow intrinsically situated as such. Now, if we look carefully, into areas like China, for example, into some South American nations and others, we find that the way we think, the way we talk and argue, from the United States and from Europe, is a little bit different, than what's happening now, as in China. And in other parts of the planet.

So therefore, there's a tendency now to produce a kind of nation-state, which is not a solid nation-state as such, but is a temporary arrangement which is called nation-state; a national principle. We find that nations are coming together, with some difficulties. China and India have a close relationship; it's not perfected. There are things that are not perfect, shall we say, in relations among some of these states.

But, what you're seeing in looking around the planet as a whole, is a development among nations, of quasi-states; they're conditional states, they're temporary states; and they're divided according to languages, and social processes and habits, and so forth. But mankind is now moving into a unity of mankind.

There are certain things that are different. We're not equally practiced in all respects on all cases, but the tendency of mankind is to come to common aims of mankind. And gradually, we will evolve into nations or groups of nations, which really becomes the planetary system. We may have different accents, we may have some different memories, historical memories, and so forth; all that is there.

Science in that sense, is the measure of a meaning of human life. That is, the meaning of the future of the person who had died, the person whose death celebrates what they had achieved for mankind. Great art, great music, great things that impassion mankind, by which means mankind is able to muster himself, to reach out and achieve necessary discoveries and practices which will improve the future of mankind as such.

But we can see already, in certain cases in South America, in some parts of Africa, in some parts of Asia, you see a process where the idea of the nation-state as being some kind of hermetic institution, is doomed—not doomed in the bad sense, but doomed in the sense of growing up: That mankind is going to grow up.

And, for example, we had the discovery by Kepler; Kepler discovered the Solar System, which meant that Earth as such, just Earth, plain Earth, is not the basis for human existence. And then we go further, and by what Kepler did in discovering the Solar System, we now find the Galactic System, which is a superior system relative to the Solar System, the old system.

And mankind now finds, man is faced with reality. For example, water: Now, the supply of water on Earth is pretty good. As a matter of fact, if we used our heads a little bit more, we would have less arid conditions, but we just haven't paid attention to things that could be improved. I mean, the control of moisture, of circulating moisture in general, around Earth, and beyond Earth, and bringing that moisture into a useful relations to conditions on Earth. That's not too well developed, but it can be.

And so, that's the kind of situation that we are living with, or we have to live with. The point is, we always have to come back to the point, that mankind's destiny is to achieve what mankind has never achieved before in terms of progress, in conditions of life, just like what Kepler did in discovering the Solar System; or what we now understand as the Galactic System. And that Earth is merely a subject, of the Solar System and the Galactic System. And other things as well in the universe.

So we have to change our values, and we have to change the way mankind *treats* mankind, because what we want to do is to bring a kind of unity of function, within the mass of the human species, with a purpose of reaching goals which have not been achieved before-

---

What you're seeing, looking around the planet as a whole, is a development among nations, of quasi-states; they're conditional states, they're temporary states. And they're divided according to languages, and social processes and habits, and so forth. But mankind is now moving into a unity of mankind.

---

hand.

I could go longer on that, but I think that, for this occasion on this timeframe, I think that's the answer.

Mankind Must Progress

Q: [followup] Excuse me, I'm still a little confused. Did you think I said "irrigation"? Because I said "immigration," and I don't think you really answered the question. I said, knowing what's going on around the world of the immigrants and the borders and all that. I don't know why it went over my head, but did you answer the question, about what would you do if you were in charge? What are the steps you would take, to control the immigration and how it would affect our politics and our economy?

LaRouche: I've been working at this goal for a number of decades. [laughs] More than a few decades. That's my business, that's my profession, as I've indicated: My profession is to cause the human species to discover principles which mankind had not previously understood. That's my approach to this. It's the only way it's going to work.

Q: [followup] Do you think the way the borders are now, they need improvement, or what would you do about that?

LaRouche: I would say a lot of improvements! But mankind—it's not a matter of improvements in this, in the sense that it's too much like statistics. And statistics are not a very good measure at all. Statistics have much exaggerated importance.

The important thing is, mankind must progress in order to achieve powers on Earth, and beyond Earth as such, as the Galaxy; and that mankind's power, or de-

velopment of power to control the Galactic process, or to influence the Galactic process as a matter of control. *That's* what the mission is.

Because we all are going to die. The question is, what is the future of mankind? If we are all going to die in our time, what's the meaning of the future of mankind, for the experience of the individual human being? And that's the question that's very rarely treated.

Q: [followup] OK, thank you.

Speed: This will be our final question for today.

Q: Good afternoon, Mr. LaRouche. My name is R——. I wrote a letter to my Congressman, and I got a response. And he sent a response, and he's for regulations, but he'd not say anything about Glass-Steagall. So I want to push this guy to go forward, to support Glass-Steagall. What do I do?

No Simple Solutions

LaRouche: You're on the right track—first of all, you're on the right track! No question about that.

What do you mean by Glass-Steagall? The problem is, if somebody treats it as some kind of a scheme, that doesn't explain anything; not really. The importance of Glass-Steagall is that mankind—or, let me go back and do something, just to make this clearer.

First of all, what's called Glass-Steagall is not really understood competently. That doesn't mean that it's wrong. It means that they don't understand what they're doing. They don't understand what they're using as an attempt to make things better for mankind in the planet. They just haven't grasped that, yet. Because they don't understand the future. That mankind's identity is intrinsically located in mankind's awareness, that is, efficient awareness, of the existence of the future.

That is to say, something which has not happened, heretofore. In other words, a discovery of fact, which has been unknown previously, and the case of Kepler, for example, same thing. Einstein, the same thing. Einstein made unique discoveries, and he was the only one who made such discoveries, within the term of his lifetime.

So the issue is mankind's creation of new, higher principles, higher than mankind had ever known before, and that man's purpose in existence is to achieve the realization of the future, in those terms. In other words, to make a discovery, which mankind had not discovered heretofore, a useful discovery, a necessary discovery; and that's what the principle is.

Now, what's happening in the schools system, for example? What's the education system in the United States today? Or, take the whole period from the beginning of the Twentieth Century on, there has been a consistent degeneration in the powers of thinking, within the policy of the people of the United States, in particular.

The people in the United States, each generation, are going through a *de*-generation! Now there may be exceptions in individual cases, but the general tendency is: for example, let's take the education in schools. The school system, the education system, both for universities as for ordinary schools, is *incompetent, intrinsically*. It's not entirely useless, but as an intention, it's useless. It does not answer the question of how mankind can progress in mankind's condition, within the Solar System, etc., etc.

So that's where the problem lies. I think the greatest criminal has been the Twentieth Century notion of science. And that notion which is commonly practiced, by people *except* for Einstein, is the folly of the United States. Look at what we do. What do we do? We are actually driving,—the average citizen, as the citizen is born and educated, the citizen in the typical case is *degenerating*. The typical person in the United States is degenerating with each generation; in other words, every 25 years. Every 25 years you get a new generation, or something like that, and every time, the person you are promoting, is more stupid, more corrupt, than the person before.

The education system is stupid, it's deliberately stupid. It's destructively stupid. The skills for production are being lost; fewer and fewer people share the powers of competence in production. We're all living under the green idea, the green policy, and the green policy is tragic destruction of the human species as a whole. But the Greenies are servants of Satan in fact, in their effect. So these are the kinds of problems that have to be considered.

And people would like to have simple things, which can be simply described, simply explained, but none of those simple things will do anything for the future of

U.S. Navy/Lt. j.g. Alexander Perrien

FLASHPOINT: Despite repeated statements by the Russians that they see the Europe-based BMD system as a threat to their national security, and the conclusion of the nuclear deal with the nominal "threat," Iran, Obama has refused to abandon the deployment. Here, the Naval Support Facility being prepared in Deveselu, Romania—which will be part of the Aegis Ballistic Missile Defense System.

mankind. We're going to Hell right now, in the United States in particular. We're going to Hell! And you look at the degeneration after generation, and generation to generation to generation; a *degeneration*, progressive degeneration, of the mental and moral life of the young generations as they come along. [applause]

Mankind's Mission—in the Galaxy

Speed: Lyn, we're at the end for today, but I want to take something up which has come up *clearly* in the discussion. I want to address it, and give you a chance, Lyn, to respond, and conclude us for the day.

What has been happening, for particularly the last two weeks, is that people are having, at least in their estimate, a helluva time getting across anything that you're basically saying about Hillary Clinton, nuclear war, etc.

Now: What's actually happening is, instead of discussing this, forthrightly and simply and straightforwardly, we get a lot of individual issues. Whether it's Puerto Rico, whether it's this, it's that, because that's what's talked about in the street. That's what people run into in the street. And then they say, "I have this question, should we do this or that?" Like this issue of immigration is another one, or many other issues. There're issue after issue after issue! People are bombarded by issues, in this and that.

Now we know, there's a term we use to—we're in

polite company, but you know, "issues" can mean, shall we say, something emanating from the posterior. And people get continually bombarded—and then they say, "but this is what's really on my mind, you're not addressing this, and I wanted to say something about this, because it's what's been represented as the problem."

Maybe people don't think that's fair. I think it's fair, because I've been in these discussions, I know what's being said. And so, I just wanted to ask you, since the Manhattan Project is your project, you've been very clear about what you wanted. You talked about us having a several-hundred person chorus; you talked about us talking to people about very difficult musical ideas. John Sigerson's here with us; we're working on these ideas, and the problem that's coming up is [whispers], "Why are we doing this?" Hmm? "Why are we doing this! Shouldn't we be talking about things which are much more issue-oriented, or practical?" etc.

So I thought I should express that to you, as we come to the close.

LaRouche: I think there are many ways I can approach this subject, so let's pick one! One of the ways, the famous formulation, "one of the ways."

Anyway! The question is, what's mankind's mission? Mankind's mission is to progress as a species. I've emphasized this already in several remarks I've made hitherto today. We have to understand, that unless you have made a discovery of a new principle, a real, true principle, a physical principle, then you haven't made any progress. As a matter of fact, if you're operating on that basis of not doing something in that way of progress, you're engaged in decadence.

I mean, for example, what happened? What happened is, with Bertrand Russell, in particular, destroyed the idea of actual science! That's what he did. And there are very few people in the United States today, who actually believe in physical science as a science. They will talk about mathematics, which means they're idiots. Because that doesn't explain anything.

The issue is mankind is distinct, in the fact that we have the power, as a species, to progress, to get more power for mankind, why? Because it's wanted. Because mankind's mission is to do that, is to make discoveries and to get along the process of trying to get ahead someplace, get ahead for mankind's future. And that is not what is taught today! What's taught today is mathematics, and mathematics is a design of evil, actually. Because what it does, it says everything can be explained by mathematics: Well, actually, almost nothing can be

attributed to mathematics as such. But that's what's taught. That's what the schools system is! That's what the education system is; there are exceptions to that, of course, but they *are* exceptions.

And therefore, the problem mankind has is: we have not met the challenge, as Kepler for example, Kepler defined the Solar System. And most people would not understand that Solar System concept. Now we understand, the Galactic System; we don't understand it perfectly, but we understand its implication of its existence, which means that mankind must *go forward* into higher layers of ability of mankind, as a species, to achieve things that mankind has never achieved before.

And that's the purpose of living! That's the purpose of life. And when you die, one hopes that you will have made a contribution to the future of mankind. That's the proper purpose. I mean, giving birth to children, human children, is what? It's a contribution to the future of mankind. It means you've got to get some kind of an education system for these children; that they give them the powers to go to a higher step upward, beyond what mankind is capable of doing today. And to take any part of the planet where you find young people, or even middle-aged people, who are rotting away at the same old, same old, same old. No future, no meaning to the future of their life.

What mankind does not have, or lacks, the sense that death is not a terrible thing; it's an inevitable thing. But the point is, what's the purpose of going through the process which leads to death, *among* human beings, *within* society? And it's the progress in developing mankind's ability *to make discoveries of physical principle*, as we call them, and those physical principles are the things on which the prosperity, of mankind as a species depends. Conquer the Galaxy, which is the challenge thrust before us, now. The major challenge of mankind today, is to understand and to better, the idea of the Galaxy, which is, so far, the thing we're best informed on, among all the things that we're not yet informed on.

But mankind's progress, in effect, in terms of the effect of the role of the human species within the Solar System and beyond, *that's* the issue! And if that's not your motive, your motive is very, very shallow! [applause]

Speed: Tough and irritating messages that are nonetheless absolutely essential. Thank you very much, Lyn, for what you had to say!

The Choral Principle versus The Zeusian Principle

by Mindy Pechenuk

If we are to win the crucial victory today, in the month of August, to stop thermonuclear war, to dump Obama, and then to create a new Presidency for the United States, and, to join with all the other nations of this world in a galactic alliance of principle among all, then it is necessary to understand what has happened to our minds and souls, since the late Nineteenth and Twentieth Century, and continuing today. Lyndon LaRouche took this up at the August 1, 2015 Saturday Dialogue with the Manhattan Project.

Modern civilization, particularly since the beginning of the Twentieth Century was a disaster for the people in Europe and the United States, as well—a moral disaster, but a moral disaster with strong characteristics, as worse things to do.

Technically, the point is, what every great musician, composer, knew, was the principle of Bach, and the principle of those who followed Bach, such as Mozart, notably, Beethoven, and so forth, up through Brahms. This was very well known. There were differences in the way they approached something, but that was not a contradiction in their effort; it was a different expression, but based on following: for example, Beethoven followed Mozart. Beethoven was followed by such great people as Brahms. Brahms ended his life within the context of the Nineteenth Century.

And then suddenly Furtwängler came along, and Furtwängler provided the means to continue the mission, which had been handed down through Brahms. In other words, Furtwängler was actually a follower, in that sense, of Brahms.

Wolfgang Amadeus Mozart (1756-1791) singing on his death bed, with musician friends, depicted by artist Thomas W. Shields.

That is, he added something to what Brahms had accomplished, and it was beyond the achievement of Brahms himself....

I now present to you the case study of Franz Liszt,[1] as a representative of the house of Zeus (Satan), whose music was created to produce the practical, deductive, mathematical, sensual man of feelings and sound. One of the many crimes of Liszt, lies not only in his own compositions, but, what he did to take compositions of great composers, like Mozart, and destroy them so you would never discover the true nature of Mozart's discovery, and Mozart's dedication to his discovery of

---

1. Mindy Pechenuk, "The Murder of Music with the Death of Brahms," *EIR*, June 12, 2015.

Bach's discovery.[2] In specific, we are going to compare Mozart's "Ave Verum Corpus," with Liszt's "Ave Verum Corpus" and Liszt's transcription of Mozart's "Ave Verum Corpus." Through the comparisons, I hope to provoke your mind to make a discovery of beauty, and of what it is to be a truly creative human soul.

Mozart's 'Ave Verum Corpus'[3]

Before we step into the world of Zeus, through Franz Liszt, think about what is in Mozart's mind— what was his mission, and intention in composing the "Ave Verum Corpus?" The "Ave Verum" was composed toward the end of Mozart's life. This is one of the most difficult compositions to sing. Why is that the case?

If your view of man, is that man is an animal, and that you live for your momentary pleasures, with no responsibility to create discoveries that have never existed before (which is the real future and the creative process) and that advance the existence of all mankind, to a higher platform of development and good within the galaxy,—then your insight into Mozart's discovery will be wrong!! That is the problem with the overwhelming number of performances, not only of this composition, but of everything else today that you hear that is called "Classical."

On the other hand, what is truly Classical, is to understand that each one of us is going to die, and what is important is what we did with that life, to contribute discoveries of new principles never discovered before, to produce and create ideas, and children, that carry the *human species* forward. In other words, your mission of life is the *choral principle*; that is, your dedication to the future of the entire species of mankind, as that is your mission for being.

Listen and compare these two different performances of the Mozart "Ave Verum Corpus:"

• West Coast Schiller Institute Performance, performed at C=256.

• Leonard Bernstein

Again, let us go back to the Saturday Dialogue with Lyndon LaRouche in Manhattan:[4]

---

2. Lyndon LaRouche's Saturday dialogue with Manhattan'
See also Megan Beets
3. See Mindy Pechenuk, *Ave Verum*, *Campaigner*, Winter 1996
See also Lyndon LaRouche on Mozart's Ave Verum
44.LaRouche's response on the Thursday, July 23, 2015 Fireside Chat:
   I think the first thing we need, is you need people who are experts in

...The point is there's a principle, the principle of music among other things—the Classical principle. Why do we say, not *on* the note? Why *between* the notes? Why do we say *between* the notes? Because the significance of music, when it's decent music, when it's good music, is that the tone is placed between the notes. That is, in the movement from one note to the next note, and so forth and so on, there's a process which identifies the meaning, the actual meaning of the performance, and the way the performance is composed. And that's the principle.

So, the problem is, that most people today, do not have any actual efficient comprehension of what that means, and unfortunately we have terrible music, and we have also terrible science. They're both incompetent. Physical science, as defined by almost everybody in the Twentieth Century and today, is rotten, from the standpoint of science, because they don't know that principle that human beings....

Yes, they do have tones; they do place tones,

---

the principles of Classical musical composition. This means, essentially, the people who are going to go through the experience, which follows the trail from the founding of Johann Sebastian Bach. Because Bach introduced a principle of composition and elaborated it somewhat in the course of his lifetime as well.

Then he had followers, such as Mozart, and Mozart was an absolute genius; and Beethoven, an absolute genius. And you had followers of these geniuses who set forth a principle of musical composition, and that principle, while it may seem complicated to some people, is actually the foundation of all competent success in the moral development which is a necessary development of the human individual; a moral development in which the student, has been educated in music and practicing music, and, first of all, has the idea of locating the voice.

In other words, if the person tries to sing the voice on the idea of trying to sing as such, they'll often fail, and they'll get into bad habits that will lead into confusion. But what has happened in the course of history, from Bach into the beginning of the Nineteenth and Twentieth Century,-the last great man was essentially, at one point was Brahms. Then you had a few people who spilled over into the Twentieth Century, and typical of course, was Furtwängler. And Furtwängler's role is typified by one example which any teacher of singing should have as a basis for approaching students—any kind of students at all ages.

And the placement of the voice is what the question is: Because the mistake that's made, which is destructive, is when you assume that the tone that you're singing, that is the indicated tone, when you base yourself on that, you get into a trap. Because Classical musical composition is based *between the notes*: That's the formal expression: *between the notes*, not *on* the notes. The notes are there, but it's the motion *between* the notes, which defines the kind of composition which is intended by all the great composers and the great performing artists....

and things like that, but that's not the answer. The answer is, what is the principle which makes a composition, of music, for example, what makes it beautiful? and what otherwise is not beautiful? And that is the placement of the tone which is *between* the notes; not *on* the notes, *between* the notes. And the fact that the orchestration of performance lies between the notes rather than on the notes. [See footnote 2]

In the case of the Leonard Bernstein's performance of the "Ave Verum Corpus"—not only is the tuning too high, which itself destroys the poetical idea, but, he performs it as if man is an animal. The singing is completely on the notes, and he is literal to the notes—creating a wall of sound that destroys your mind and soul. From Bernstein's performance you get his world view: that when an individual dies, all dies with him. Bernstein's view of man and music is completely that of an animal. Mozart would be very upset, with the way Bernstein has destroyed the knowability of the immortal nature of man's willful creation of the future. Go back to the recording by Bernstein: the end is death for him; there is no higher order resolution upward.

Listen again to the Schiller Institute performance. While it is not perfect, the tuning is C=256, and the "between-the-notes" development of Mozart is attempted. We were working to be true to Mozart's intention, and the development of his discovery of the Future—the creative process of the human mind!

The case of Franz Liszt's 'Ave Verum Corpus'

For our purposes here, I am not going to go into the history of Franz Liszt, since I want to deal directly with the subjective nature of his Zeusian satanic view of man, as it permeates the music itself—this existential, deductive, sensual wallowing in sound, for sound itself.

Now, compare Mozart's "Ave Verum Corpus "with Franz Liszt's "Ave Verum Corpus."

Franz Liszt (1811-1886) at the piano in the year of his death, 1886.

- Schiller Institute—Mozart
- Liszt: Stuttgart Sudfunk Choir

Ask yourself—what is the difference between the two views of man, and of the immortality of our species,—the critical principle of the future? Mozart's "Ave" is a beautiful example of *Motivführung*-of a thoroughly composed composition. (See footnote 3.) There is a higher order metaphor in Mozart's mind, which is driven from the future. Therefore, the composition has a unified mission, which lies between the notes, and is unfolding in a non-sequential directionality.

Mozart demands, both of the performer, and the listener, that their minds are with him in the future, in his discovery, and the "in mortis examine" at the end, is a resolution upward of the whole human species, having resolved the tension of what it is to be a responsible creative being. This led by the basses, unfolding the last "in mortis."

Ave Verum Corpus

Ave, ave verum corpus
natum de Maria virgine,
vere passum immolatum
in cruce pro homine.
Cuius latus perforatum
unda fluxit et sanguine,
esto nobis praegustatum
in mortis examine.

Hail, hail true body,
born of the virgin Mary,
truly having suffered sacrifice
on the cross on behalf of man.
Whose pierced side
trickled water and blood
be thou for us a foretaste
in the test of death.

Schiller Institute

Author Mindy Pechenuk conducts the West Coast Schiller Institute chorus in the "Ave Verum Corpus," November 14, 2103.

Take the opening, and then the closing, of both Mozart and Liszt:

• Example 1—the opening of the Mozart (measures 1-10); the beginning of the recording to 45 seconds;

• Example 2—the opening of the Liszt (measures 1-10); from the beginning to 44 seconds;

• Example 3—measures 30 to the end of the Mozart; from 2:10 to 3:34 in the recording; and

• Example 4—measures 31 to the end of the Liszt; from 2:17.

In Mozart's case, he composes a fundamental paradox, between the intervals and notes, which is why he repeats the "Ave" twice. For Mozart, this discovery is what we can call the "Lydian Principle." Mozart has in his mind the discovery he made from J.S. Bach, singing between the notes, and the creation of multi-ordered modalities, such as those the Lydian principle unfolds. Thus, Mozart continues shifting your mind and soul upward, until the end of this short work, where you do resolve a future for humanity.

What does Liszt compose? A wall of chromaticism, which endlessly drones on throughout the composition, creating a non-creative tension, in which, by the end of the composition, everything dies when you die. Once you enter the wall of chromaticism, and the

higher tuning, the very crucial principle of tuning the mind is gone. Missing are the higher orders of mind, which are the domain where the tuning between the notes occurs, and the placement of the mind/voice as a one!!

This distinction between chromaticism, and the Lydian principle is crucial. It represents the difference between mathematical deduction of the mind, and the truth about the beauty of man discovering the higher hypothesis of his mind developing his universe. As the intergalactic affects the galaxy, and the galactic, the Solar System!

One last example—Liszt's transcription of Mozart "Ave Verum Corpus:"

Compare Liszt's transcription of Mozart "Ave Verum" to the Schiller Institute's performance of Mozart's "Ave Verum."

Think of the difference between the two!! The difference is the fate of mankind—the difference between thermonuclear war, and a real Renaissance. There has been too much beauty from Plato, to Cusa, to Kepler, Bach, Mozart, Brahms, Furtwängler et al., to let it be destroyed in an instant. Let us embrace the true nature of the future, into our minds and souls, and rise to the challenge.

www.ingramcontent.com/pod-product-compliance
Lightning Source LLC
Chambersburg PA
CBHW052042280526

45791CB00010B/3045